ORGANIZE WITH (

For a complete list of Management Books 2000 titles
visit our web-site on http://www.mb2000.com

ORGANIZE WITH CHAOS

**PUTTING MODERN CHAOS THEORY TO WORK
IN YOUR OWN ORGANISATION**

**A NEW SCIENCE PERSPECTIVE OF BUSINESS,
MANAGEMENT AND CHANGE**

Robin M Rowley
Joseph J Roevens

2000

First edition published 1996

This new edition published 2007 by
Management Books 2000 Ltd
Forge House, Limes Road
Kemble, Cirencester
Gloucestershire, GL7 6AD, UK
Tel: 0044 (0) 1285 771441
Fax: 0044 (0) 1285 771055
E-mail: info@mb2000.com
Website: www.mb2000.com

Printed and bound in Great Britain by The Good News Press, Ongar

British Library Cataloguing in Publication Data is available

ISBN 9781852525613

'...the basic laws of nature as formulated by Newton...describe a timeless, deterministic universe...In recent years we have witnessed a radical change in perspective. On all levels from cosmology to biology, we discover instabilities, and fluctuations, which lead to evolutionary patterns...We obviously need a different formulation of physics which includes instability and chaos and is in agreement with the evolutionary world in which we are embedded.'

Ilya Prigogine, The End of Certainty, 1997

To 'Organize' means: 'to furnish with living organs; make organic; make into a living being or tissue.'

The Concise Oxford Dictionary, 5th Edition

This book is dedicated to all of our friends.

*We take full responsibility for any credit,
and we cheerfully accept all of the blame.*

Contents

Introduction

'....a state of chaos is a state of health....It's not that scary at all.' [a]
Rudy Rucker

'In times of change, an organisation must change constantly... to keep its identity' [b]
Fritjof Capra

---

[a] 'Chaos', *Mondo2000-User's Guide to the New Edge*, Harper Collins, 1992, pp42-5
[b] during 'Systems Thinking in Management' at Schumacher College in 1992

The Greenfield Scenario

Our purpose in writing this book, is to give you a practical organisational tool to change people's behavior and habits, and also to reveal a new way for you to prospect your own organisation for new levels of performance, commitment and innovation. The book should take you only a few hours to read and to absorb. To start to write it, back in 1994, we practically had to re-consider the whole subject of business organisation. We used what Rob Kuijpers[a], then CEO of DHL Europe & Africa NV, called 'A Greenfield Scenario' and started out with a clean sheet, to test many of the existing assumptions and current practices of management and organisation. When your market environment is hostile, or it starts changing fast, that's no bad thing to do.

It is gratifying for us in this edition, to know that much of what we wrote then still holds and can now be expanded, to incorporate what has now become common executive reality. We are still discovering that so much traditional management thinking about people and organisation, particularly the need to over-control, is quite obsolete for today's volatile business conditions. Although we do try to explain why throughout the text, our first objective is to offer you a practical, if sometimes radical, new way to recognise and to deal in practice with the changes affecting your business.

We refer to several businesses cases which exemplify this new approach to organisations. Often we purposely omit the name, the country of origin or even the date of the case's occurence. This is because we consider much good management practice to be independent of national culture, time or history.

---

[a] In 2002 Kuijpers was asked to help the upstart SN Brussels Airlines as its CEO, and in April 2005 also the Virgin Express airlines. Since December 2005 he presides Aviapartner, a freight carrier.

11

This is not a technique, or a recipe book however. It is a lens. This lens will enable you to look deeply inside the processes of modern business and organisational change, and to view unfolding events from a fresh perspective. Change is not static. An informed, more dynamic model of the change process is urgently required, in order to make sense of today's fast changing business environment. To shape this new lens, we have borrowed heavily from many fields of knowledge. We hope that it will enable you to welcome and to understand our unstable and chaotic business world in a new way.

In modern science, as well as in business, the days of predictability and certainty are over. As we approach the end of the twentieth century, it can come as a shock for many executives to realise just how far, even a hard science like Physics, has moved away from the static engineering view of reality, which most of us learned at school and which still governs so much managerial thinking. Last year for example, we were invited to speak on the platform of a new-science executive seminar in Brussels. For many of the managers and consultants at that meeting it was a jaw dropping experience, especially when one speaker, the distinguished scientist and Nobel laureat Ilya Prigogine, quite casually remarked that in his view of Physics today '...material and physical reality (the very stuff of which we are made) is just one aspect of probability'!

Probability, irreversible luck and random accident has entered the equations of science. In conventional management and organisation, we do not welcome such random chaotic factors, because they cannot be determined or controlled, and can wreck our carefully designed strategic plans. However in recent years, for most of us, the experience of business reality itself has fundamentally changed. Our root assumptions about the nature of this reality must also change, if we are to be able to deal with it effectively. Things are no longer static today, nor is change incremental, it is too often discontinuous and quite unexpected. Adaptive flexibility must somehow be incorporated into modern organisation design. The question for any business person today is how can you possibly set up and run an efficient profitable organisation and also simultaneously manage to change, to cope with today's uncertainty?

Our research tells us that a lot depends on how you see things, or how you frame such a paradoxical situation. Conventional thinking puts you in an either/or dilemma. It insists, for example, that you either reduce costs, *or*, you invest for growth; you either organise for tighter efficiency, *or* you loosen up for creativity and innovation., but not both. New scientific business thinking however is either/and; it admits paradox. It's about being able to do both efficiency *and* innovation simultaneously, and to execute both superbly well. Those kinds of assumptions are rooted in the model of science that guides the way that you were taught to think. Basically, if you think that something is impossible, you are right. For you it is impossible. That's the trouble with conventional linear organisational thinking, it limits you. In business, there is in fact only one valid either/or scenario. It is simply stated, either you make money, or you will eventually go bust.

It is often the unexpected which contains the seeds of both opportunity and potential catastrophe. Unpredictable events and emerging new trends must be spotted quickly, shared across many organisational functions, and then decisively acted upon. To be able to get such rapid organised cooperation on a large scale, organisational change must evolve from within the people. An internal culture which promotes the open and free exchange of information is crucial. In the shifting global information based markets of today, this either means survival and new growth, or rapid obsolescence and extinction. And each scenario can begin to happen fast, and with little warning.

In both cases, rapid growth or impeding obsolescence, will inevitably produce large scale organisational chaos. Any internal resistance to change will inevitably compound that chaos. The organisational challenge is not to deny, nor to fight, or to try to control business chaos. It is to understand and to employ its unique properties. Blame and excuses are out. We have to learn how to put chaos to work, as a creative energising force for sustained health and renewal in our business organisations. Rather than being written off as just another road kill victim of the unexpected, who couldn't respond fast enough, we should aim to join the market leaders, whose remarkable success generates chaos for others in our industry. Change efficiency is a competitive issue today.

Today, any determined little firm, located anywhere, which is equipped with a computer, a modem and a telephone line, can seriously join and wreak havoc in the global market place. And that's exactly what is now happening, all over the world. Large organisations are under constant threat from agile and resourceful upstarts, which can appear out of nowhere. Big businesses are being compelled to adapt and change themselves constantly, to cope with this relentless hostile change pressure, on a 24-hour basis. The unpredictability of the new economy demands a radical new model of business organisation.

The linear machine models of organisation which have been successfully used in management for decades, don't work where such large scale changes are involved. They were actually designed to control and resist chaos, at a time when the world markets were in the protective hands of a few big players. Linear thinking works for closed, predictably stable systems, but not for open-ended complexity and change of this magnitude. These rigid models of certainty and predictability are not based on current scientific awareness. This book attempts to correct that view, and to transfer and translate some fundamentally new insight and scientific literacy over to business people at any level.

The departmental walls are coming down fast in business management, and people will often feel vulnerable and exposed, being out of their own comfort zone. The point is you've just got to go out to really do your best, and learn as much as you can on the way. Unlike the time of the Renaissance, no one person can be an expert in everything today. We know ourselves, as authors and public speakers, how scary it can feel standing alongside world class scientists, knowing that you're way out of your field. Of course, you do your homework, but you still hope that no specialist is going to try to attack you over the details. You've got to expect a few setbacks today, it's healthy. When you go beyond some people's comfort zones, you will invariably get resistance, so expect it. Also the specialised language of other disciplines can take serious mental chewing. For what we've learned so far, it's worth taking the trip. The technical capability to share information at all levels is driving all of us out of our own specialised fields, status positions and former roles in business today. If we use it to encourage diversity and to get as much of the whole picture as we all can, this can liberate new strategic insight to emerge and resonate, from anywhere in the organisation. This journey is the learning.

> '*The internet is the most important single development to come along since the IBM PC was introduced in 1981...The impetus for Microsoft's response to the internet didn't come from me or from our other senior executives. It came from a small number of dedicated employees who saw events unfolding...they were able to rally everybody to their cause...smart people anywhere in the company should have the power to drive an initiative.*' [a]
>
> Bill Gates

This book looks at change from a Senior Executive's Perspective. As Bill Gates' example illustrates above, it is obvious that the real dynamics of a major change, must at least be understood by those people with executive power in an organisation, otherwise the evolution of any fresh initiatives can easily be killed prematurely. We will talk in some detail about what executives should *not* do if they seriously wish to empower their people to self-organise and to take active control of their individual and collective destiny.

Organisations only change when people change and no one is

---

[a] 'The Day Microsoft 'Got' the Internet', *The Financial Times*, 19/3/99, p18

exempted. The first job is to prime a new organisational change-culture in your firm. This book should provide a modern manager at any level with a basic tool kit to do this, and getstarted . It will also give you guidance to understand and monitor the dynamics of change, in real-time, as it happens. Basically, we want you to be able to start well, and then be able to handle the shifting architecture of a modern business transformation, much more comfortably, effectively, and also safely.

Some ideas are freshly imported into management from other subject disciplines. Others are based on a careful sifting of the published best modern business practices that we could get hold of. These are proven methods, but could not be understood and transferred, using the old classical organisational context. To save you time, we have tried to cut through much of the confusion and theoretical complexity which surrounds the literature and vocabulary of business change, and to strip things down to a few simple key elements and relationships. Let us start early and begin to tell you a little of what has emerged from our research.

'Evolutionary design is healthier than visionary design.'[a]
Stewart Brand

We wanted to understand more about how things evolve and change in nature, so we looked into Biology and Paleo-Anthropology, and asked the question:

'How do natural life forms spontaneously change and adapt?'

An examination of human evolution and other living forms of temporal adaptation, indicated that four quite distinct 'phases' or 'dimensions' were at work, which to us, seemed to provide a useful way to classify, or group, the spontaneous change process.

This is what happens in such un-managed cases:

---

[a] Stewart Brand, *How Buildings Learn*, Penguin, 1994, p221

- Something major changes in the environment. The old ways stop working.

- Confusion reigns and individual variations and mutations are pragmatically tested.

- Small adaptive differences and luck favours the survival of some new types.

- These surviving differences act across populations, reproducing a new breed or species.

If we then apply these spontaneous evolutionary dynamics, in an intelligent effort to change a manageable system like a human organisation, it becomes apparent that we can sometimes intervene to promote, to sustain or even to accelerate the process, but great care must be exercised, because we can also inadvertently collapse the change process too. It is often the dimensional context in which an intervention is made, which can make all the difference between success and failure. Sometimes it's better for a manager to feel comfortable and just back off and do nothing, the question is when?

Where direct intervention and the intelligent management of change is involved, we had to borrow a few process concepts from modern Chaos Theory. The way that, for example, unpredictability, spontaneous self-organisation and attractor outcomes contribute to the complete lens will be discussed at greater length later in the book. For now, we ask you only to consider and distinguish between the spontaneous unmanageable aspects, and the manageable aspects, which together, comprise four major dimensions of organisational change. When the possibility of management intervention exists, these four dimensions of change will then look like this:

- Enhance   Environmental change-pressure is detected, and felt.

- Perturb   Existing routines fail, and diverge into creative turbulence and chaos.

- Attract   Fresh diversity emerges; a few feeble sensitivities survive and grow.

- Excite   Synergy and clusters converge to shape an effective new 'critical mass'.

Although changing systems will pass through each dimensional form, direct management intervention can only really be made to Enhance and Excite, the process. The right things done at the wrong time can easily collapse or inhibit a changing system's evolution.The other two self-organising aspects of change, defy external manipulation or massage.

Left to its own devices, a changing system will appear to spontaneously Perturb itself, as each individual or group attempts or fails, to successfully adapt. In nature, the change process releases all manner of strange variations and geek mutations, but will Attract only those few pragmatic outcomes which work, and thus survive the experiment. In the two truly evolutionary dimensions of Perturb and Attract, deliberate under-management, recognition and democratic protection is a far better executive strategy.

Deeper into the book, some suggested 'steps' will be proposed, which are in coherent phase relationship to each other, and are also linked holistically, to the whole transformational change process. It is important for you to know at the start, how the first actions that you take, can fit into the overall scheme. You can then recognise and trace their movements and outcomes early. Understanding the change-dimension, or scenario, within which the evolution of each action is playing out, may help you to know what to do, and it will certainly indicate what not to do, until the situation gets ripe.

We have bench tested the complete lens in a series of interviews with a variety of practising Executives, ranging from Personnel Managers to CEO's, since our first edition. Aspects of the lens have been practically and successfully applied in various organisational settings, ranging from small to medium-sized corporations, and to MBA educational processes. So far, most of the people who 'get it' tell us that it simplifies things and makes practical sense. We hope that you will find it useful too.

Insights and metaphors have been incorporated from modern Physics, Biology, World Philosophy and the new Psychologies of Choice, Entrepreneurship and Healing, because that's where the process of change is best understood today. What has emerged from this universal melting pot is a simple, practical new perspective on the subject of business and organisational transformation. Any enduring quality to this work lives in what survived, measured against what we threw out. We urge you to mine this book for fresh ideas, and to use anything here that makes common sense to you.

If you've got a change problem, or a change opportunity at the moment, read this little book.

Part 1

CHAOS IS THE RULE, NOT THE EXCEPTION

In this section we will explain to you how the business environment is radically changing, and why this requires a fundamentally new way to begin to see and understand the unpredictable dynamics of organisations and organisational change. In the first chapter we explain what chaos is, and present some of the characteristic dynamics of a chaotic environment. In the second chapter we critically describe the key assumptions and elements of several popular change methods, and we show why many of them are inappropriate for today's unstable non-linear business conditions.

1

Change Begins with Acceptance

'There is order within the disorder of chaos. That order is self-similarity, regular-irregularity, (and) a constant degree of variability.' [a]

Ralph Stacy

The modern scientific concept of chaos is generally misunderstood. The public, the media and many executives, still use the word chaos to describe a mess, a disaster or a situation of unbridled anarchy. A few years ago *The Economist* published a cartoon story, entitled 'Econoclast vs Dr. Chaos'. In this story the hero, Mr. Econoclast – a superficial metaphor for the average conservative, capitalist economist – fights the bad guy, Dr. Chaos – a business-monster who creates havoc in world markets. In this fable Mr. Econoclast, a rational control freak, wins. Chaos literates know that in reality he never would. They know that without chaos, there is in fact no possibility for life, never mind the opportunity to create order. Chaos is not a mess, nor is it pure randomness or disaster.

In modern science the word chaos describes the fine ingrained patterns of order which exist in most kinds of natural, or stochastic disorder. We use the term chaos in this sense. As a scientific newcomer, chaos is still a misunderstood and undervalued feature of mental and physical health. Chaos is the essence of all living systems, which actually need a degree of chaos and irregularity in

---

[a] *The Chaos Frontier*, Butterworth Heineman, 1991, p170

23

order to stay healthy. Chaos is ubiquitous and natural. You'll find chaos in your own heartbeat, in the neural activities of your brain, as well as in the organisms studied in biology, and in the material and energy flows of modern physics and chemistry.

'We can use the resulting self similar pattern of winter weather to prepare appropriate behaviour – we can buy an umbrella or move the sheep off the high ground...in a qualitative way...humans are mentally equipped to deal with chaos.' [a]

Ralph Stacy

Chaos is also firmly embedded in human perception and behavior. It is the key to pattern recognition and adaptive, creative behaviour. Once you know more about chaotic systems, you will see them everywhere. For now, just think deeply about your own business. Do you know of any company, or organisation that does not in fact know chaos? The practical challenge for any executive today is not so much to try to fight and eliminate Chaos, but to learn to understand and to use it strategically, as a vital creative resource.

Chaos Theory is a child of the computer. Without the computer, scientists could not have run the original simple non-linear equations, that today model and describe the behaviour of complex, non-linear chaotic systems. One of the principal developers of chaos theory, Edward Lorenz, built a simple mathematical weather model and discovered 'fractals' after letting his computer calculate and graph the interaction of a few simple non-linear equations, all through the night! He saw how small differences in the initial decimal values put through these equations, quickly amplified and completely transformed the inter-active behaviour of the whole system. In far from equilibrium systems like the weather or stock markets, tiny differences at the start of the process will produce a different Fractal outcome.

---

[a] ibid, p166

A Fractal is a geometric picture of the shaping behaviour of a chaotic system's deep architecture, over time. Like a Hologram, each part of a Fractal is a reduced scale version of the whole. When magnified, a Fractal will reveal a massively complex pattern of order, which repeats again and again. These patterns are similar to each other, but they are never exactly the same. Fractals look incredibly natural. Some resemble intricate cloud formations, others look like the ripples on a windswept pool, or the growth patterns of a leaf or a snowflake. Fractals emerge as outcomes, around what scientists call the system's 'strange' or chaotic 'Attractors'.

When you examine the behaviour of an open living system like a business organisation from such a scientifically informed perspective, the dynamics get so complicated so quickly, that predictability is impossible. All possible scenarios will quickly diverge in time. The sensitivity of such a system to initial conditions, means that infinitesimally small events, particularly at the start of any intervention, really do matter. Few certainties exist in science today and the often dramatic effects of random irreversible luck can never be predicted. Also the term 'Attractor' itself is misleading. Attractors are not magnetic and their Fractal patterned outcomes cannot be determined by the kind of linear cause' and effect' logic that most of us learned at school. This is not such a difficult idea to tolerate however. In sports like soccer and ice hockey, the goal post does not magnetically attract the ball. A scored goal is simply recognised as just one outcome in the complex holistic inter-action of the play. We will say more about the practical management of this kind of uncertainty, later.

Chaos alone contains higher order potential. Like the ancient Chinese symbol for crisis, it is pregnant with potential opportunity and also with potential disaster. Learning how to deal effectively with business chaos is becoming an inevitable new management skill today. This is not suprising. When its life supporting environment changes suddenly, any purposeful organism, or business organisation, which depends on that environment, must be able to adapt. When these environmental changes are

25

fundamental, creative adaptation is required. This often means a journey into the unknown. If it is to survive, the organisation unit must leave its former state of ordered structure and efficient habits, pass through a turbulent unpredictable phase of creative experimental chaos, and then begin to harvest the new fruits of ripe chaos and to efficiently bring them to market.

Only that which emerges well adapted from the chaos test may survive and grow, into a new benchmark' state of higher order performance, or novelty. Rigid inflexibility and the inability to adapt and change along with the environment, condemns an organisation to the scrapyards of disintegration and premature extinction. Paradoxically, if order and control is imposed on the system at the wrong time, the self-organising process of change will collapse and it will die. In practice this usually means protecting the young fresh upstarts and helping them to avoid any powerful, but hostile internal change resistance. The interference from former, or current, successful ways of doing things, must be emasculated, limited, or be fundamentally challenged, absorbed and changed. In the long term, the real danger of not continuously adapting to the shifts in the modern business climate, is that the whole organisation can and will become unstable and probably disappear. Management today must be considered as a continuous experiment.

Nature experiments by throwing a whole lot of diversity into a changing environment. Most of her experiments actually fail. Adaptive success and long-term stability in business today is likewise built on how you handle failure. It takes a whole string of small experimental risks, mistakes and failures, orchestrated in permanent dis-equilibrium, to ensure the overall system's adaptive stability. When things are changing fast out there, only a creative strategy of widespread institutional chaos will prevent total systemic collapse!

Once you understand this paradox, you can begin to learn to love change as much as you used to hate it. In business today, chaos is the rule, not the exception. The Chaos Theory metaphor is not a management fad. It represents a fundamental shift in how scientists view the nature of our material and psychic reality. Change only begins with acceptance. We believe that understanding and accepting chaos conceptually is an important first step towards modern management education. This new scientific discovery offers a great opportunity for executives to interpret and to deal effectively, with what is happening in the global business world of today.

In recent decades, a business organisation could still afford to plan and to move slowly; to set modest incremental goals, and to centre itself around a tight, control-oriented bureaucracy. This system of organisation was in fact designed to fight chaos. It seeks efficiency not innovation and, because it requires a whole chain of 'yes's' before something new can happen, it can only change itself slowly. One 'no' in the chain will shoot down any new project. Today's environment no longer tolerates such organised sluggishness. So what is different today? Let us now identify some of the most important background forces and events, which weave through the new environmental tapistry, and upon which any business depends. Here's a checklist of some typically new environmental sources of modern business chaos:

- Higher customer expectations; their new buying habits, and the trend of customers sharing information on your performance, set against your competitor's alternatives.

- Rapid technological innovation and obsolescence of existing products and services,

- Cross-cultural misunderstandings.

- Rapid organisational growth and extinctions in some business units.

- More stringent environmental legislation and increased customer awareness.

- Talent bleeding and specific skill shortages.

27

- Volatile world stock-markets.

- Newtonian consultants.

Today's customers have rapid access to much more crucial information than 1970s customers did. On line, they can compare price, service and quality almost globally. Moreover, they are becoming accustomed to higher standards of service. For example, only a few years ago, Europeans had to wait for weeks for a new telephone connection from the national telephone monopoly. Today, with de-regulation, if a customer is dissatisfied, they can just ask another telecom provider to serve them. Likewise, the national postal services are under attack from the swifter, more agile and customer friendly, private parcel delivery carriers.

As consultants Hagel & Armstrong explained in their book 'Net Gain', the World Wide Web is also dramatically shifting the balance of marketing power away from producers and advertisers, towards virtual communities of customers and enthusiasts.

On the Internet, you don't sell product, you build community. An effective web-marketing strategy starts with the creation of a Virtual Community. This VC – in Webtalk – accretes around active interesting sites, that your potential customer traffic may choose to visit. Here, they will both obtain, and also provide uncensored information among each other about you and also your competitors.

The purpose of the VC is not to sell products or services in the short run. It often gives free information to attract as much customer traffic as possible. A good site can be bookmarked and stored by a contented visitor. This has a lock-in habit effect. Once the number of regular customer / member visits reaches critical mass, the greater the lock-in and the lower the site cost. The sites become the new platform, or the next operating standard. The web breeds loyalty. If your firm has got its web act together early, then customers who naturally choose to stop and sometimes shop at your Website, will tell others and probably remain with you in the long run. These new dynamics represent a strategic shift away from short term 'hit & run' marketing, to long term 'life-time value' customers.

Initially it will cost you to set up or to sponsor a Virtual Community, but as more members join, the marginal costs drop. Once you reach a critical mass of members, then you become the leading Website for that particular business sector. You become thé place to surf towards, to find out about books, or motorcycles or cheap flights to SE Asia, etc. Your site becomes the standard, the 'Microsoft' of your business. Then it's your time for big and continuous market share and profits! Also a new breed of 'Infomediary' businesses have emerged. Their search engines constantly scour the internet's product offerings, comparing price, quality and service. They then pass this information over to prospective buyers, recommending the best deals, and pick up a percentage, a fee, or advertising revenue.

'I think most people are overestimating where the Internet will be in two years, but underestimate where it will be in ten years.'

Bill Gates, 1998

Several years ago Amazon.com, 'Earth's Biggest Bookstore' didn't even exist. Nowadays it's a household name web-world-wide! People can join the Amazon website to talk about books with others, and to compare prices.

Today, to an increasingly large extent, customers can even decide how much they want to pay and how they want their books delivered. Our Antwerp distributors told us recently about some web-savvy customers buying the first edition of *Organize With Chaos* from Amazon in Seattle, rather than from the local book-chain stores, because it was faster to get hold of, and cheaper!

'Word of mouth is incredibly powerful online; a dissatisfied customer can tell 1000 people in minutes...I tell my employees that they shouldn't be afraid of our competitors – they are not the ones who give us money. They should be afraid of our customers.'

Jeffrey Bezos – Amazon.com, founder.

Not understanding the tidal wave which has engulfed and transformed how business is done, means that your firm risks exposing its core business to attack from absolute newcomers, and it will happen before you even find out about it. The web can create huge internal cost savings and generate synergies within a business. For example, by pooling all of their combined operating purchases, the separate GE businesses were able to collectively negotiate a 20% reduction on $1 billion of regular supplies.

Some CEOs still do not know much about the shift from supply chains to supply networks, where for example trucking companies can tap directly into your ordering system to plan their future schedules, or potential customers can bypass the Sales Department and tap directly into your business's inventories. One firm, Micro Age Inc. even offers its own customers information on the inventories of its rivals, when it is out of stock itself! Their information strategy is clearly focused on winning total customer loyalty. They realize that to do great business on the Internet, firms must radically switch their strategic allegiance over to serve the needs of buyers first, sometimes even sacrificing its own products.

If your product offering is not world class, customers will say bad uncensored things about your price, your service or your quality, and if they are in an influential chat-group you are in big trouble. But, once you are loved by the favourite VC's, most customers will probably stay loyally with you.

'Like automobiles, the telephone and rock music, the internet will become an indelible fixture of modern life. Not so much because we can't live without it, but because we won't want to.' [a]

Steven Levy

---

[a] *Newsweek*

Technological innovation and rapid obsolescence of existing products and services.

In 1997 the shelf life of a typical PC was 12 to 18 months. After that time the unit was obsolete. By 1999 this had fallen to six months and, because of rapid innovation, especially among the chip makers, PC shelf life will continue to shorten and drop faster. In 1996 Honda could already take a car from design to production in 6 months, against an industry standard of 2 to 3 years!

'Is your firm reacting to market chaos, or responsible for producing that chaos, by innovation.'
Ed McCracken, CEO, Silicon Graphics

Who is creating the chaos in your industry? If your competitors are making your products obsolete before you do, this will generate a lot of chaos in your markets, which may precipitate the urgent need for rapid intervention and sudden changes in your organisation. Management by crisis will rule each working day. Today's business organisations do not need a one-time 'change-fix', but must develop and grow towards continuous 'change efficiency'™, just to stay in business. In this age of global information and outsourcing, product superiority can often be easily copied. Organisational superiority and adaptive flexibility gives you a real sustainable advantage today, because it cannot be replicated so easily.

Rapid organisational growth in some business units

Highly successful companies, especially those in Information Technology, Telecoms,or Parcel Delivery Services, know double-digit growth each year. Growth often requires more people, more advanced technology, or a mix of both. People have to learn, or to

31

be educated, to continually welcome and adjust to newcomers and to new technology. This results in a state of more or less permanent dis-equilibrium and widespread institutional chaos. Even traditional companies such as the big pharmaceutical giants experience annual growth of more than 10% . You need an adaptive system of organisation, and a culture that can embrace, absorb and work comfortably with high levels of uncertainty, to really be able to deal with rapid growth effectively.

Cross-cultural misunderstandings

'There are two ways of spreading light. Either to be the candle, or the mirror which reflects it.'

Edith Wharton

There is no universal global culture yet. People from different countries or ethnic groups do not think the same way, nor are their decisions based on the same values. A short study of cross-cultural psychology makes this clear. Yet many companies have suffered unnecesary financial disasters by assuming that others think, act and consume the same as they do. A typical example is Disney, whose EuroDisney operation suffered at least a $1 billion loss due to the cultural mismatch between an American product and marketing strategy, imposed on an essentially French customer and workforce group.

Here are a few more amusing examples:

* When General Motors introduced the 'Chevy Nova' in South America, it was apparently not aware that 'no va' means it won't go. After the company figured out why it wasn't selling any cars, they changed the name to 'Caribe' for the Spanish markets.

* Scandinavian vacuum manufacturer Electrolux used the following slogan in an American advertising campaign – 'Nothing sucks like an Electrolux'.

32

- In Taiwan, the translation of the Pepsi slogan 'Come alive with the Pepsi generation' came out at first as 'Pepsi will bring your ancestors back from the dead'.

More stringent environmental legislation and increased customer awareness

One of Greenpeace's founders, Dr. Patrick Moore, left the organisation to become an independent environmental consultant. He introduced himself to a prospective client and advised its executives to improve environmental standards. When these executives asked him why they should concern themselves with this, he answered that:

> '...you can apply environmental standards now and gain a competitive advantage. Or, you can do nothing and wait until legislation and/or consumer groups close you down!'

Changes in customers' social and political awareness plus direct eco-political activism, will create new business chaos in some industries and opportunity in others. The Body Shop franchising empire now part of l'Oreal has rapidly grown by seeing (and shaping) this massive global awareness trend as a new business opportunity, and not a threat. The Body Shop actually sells animal protection and socio-environmental concern, not perfume and soap. Its loyal customers feel that this is important to support.

Talent bleeding and skill shortages

Do profits come before people in your organisation? The keeping and developing of a loyal core workforce should not be underestimated. One common result of downsizing is that many talented people leave, while the mediocre performers and astute political manipulators stay on board. It is the whole organisation and not the individuals within it, that must compete. You cannot run a business full of under-achievers and smart politicians.

There is an emerging trend among young MBA people who, having seen the corporate career carnage of the past twenty years, want to become their own boss. These new corporate entrepreneurs may decide to temporarily join, or to leave your firm, but take note, these people are not career employees. They'll be thinking and acting more like independent suppliers, as they compare various contract offers.

If such a lack of reciprocal corporate loyalty and mutual trust gets in among your core employees, it can create profound de-stabilising havoc. That's the price of ruthless cost cutting, on people. Your organisation's robustness to withstand shocks and to weather future environmental changes, depends a lot on the goodwill and focused core values of your existing people. Practical flexibility always requires some slack in the system. An over zealous, purely rational re-engineering programme, often leaves a hollowed out' inflexible shell of a firm. You don't cut for sustainable profits, you grow them. People who make money are more important than the people who count it. This means that you must invest in your own people's ability to grow the profits, if you intend to stay in business.

Volatile stock markets

'...an extraordinary acceleration of history...in every area events are unfolding at a relentless pace. Discontinuity and contradictions fuel the sense of uncertainty and confusion.'
Carlo de Benedetti, Chairman of Ing. C. Olivetti

Experts in the behavior of the financial markets see the Asian crisis, followed by the recent problems in Brazil, as evidence of the strong interdependence and frailty of the global economy. Benoit B. Mandelbrot, a mathematician and a former researcher in IBM, has been tracking the movements of the world stock markets over the years, by looking closely at the numbers. In one typical case he observed that:

'...the stocks for Alcatel, a French telecommunications equipment manufacturer, dropped about 40 percent one day and fell another six percent over the next few days. In a reversal, the stock shot up ten percent on the fourth day. The classical financial models used for most of this century predict that such precipitous events should never happen.'[a]

This scientist has developed a chaos based fractal geometry, to model the unpredictable behaviour of the global economic system. The world's financial markets are chaotic. They resemble natural evolving weather systems, coastlines, or even the pattern of the galaxies, far more than traditional economic models would care to admit.

Newtonian consultants

'The sobering truth is that our theories, models and conventional wisdom combined appear no better at predicting an organisation's ability to sustain itself than if we were to rely on random chance.'[b]

Richard Pascale

Unfortunately, many scientifically illiterate consulting firms, are actually the disease of which they pretend to be the cure. Their expensive advice is often based on lethal archaic 'scientific' assumptions. We have on file evidence from one large chain store type consulting firm, that provides change by formula. They claimed in writing that:

'We are bringing predictability and precision to the implementation of large scale business change.'

[Reference available on request.]

This particular firm also claimed that the chief executive's:

---

[a] Benoit B. Mandelbrot, "A Multifractal Walk Down Wall Street", *Scientific American*, February 1999, p50
[b] Richard Pascale, *Managing On The Edge*, Penguin, 1991, p22

'...vision is the strange attractor...a mechanism for continuous feedback...like...an autopilot system in people and organisations...if people understand the strange attractor...they'll end up at their destination...although change is about journeys, it is not about destinations...now that's chaos.'

Let's examine this teleological (design) understanding of chaos theory:

- Predictability has been replaced in science by probability and luck. You cannot predict the behaviour of a non-linear system like the business environment.

- There is no precision. On close inspection, Change is messy.

- It's not mechanical. All the computing power in the world can't even calculate and predict the path of one single falling leaf.

- You cannot understand a strange Attractor. It's an outcome not a cause, and it's certainly not magnetic.

A basic understanding of chaos theory shows this firm's claim to be nonsense. Because of change, the role of order is changing too. Too much order, predictability and regularity kills living systems. Too little room for chance and coincidence kills practical creativity and the ability to adapt. Too much worry, stress and overwork, kills people. Advocating more external interference, more measured control, and more rational hard 'engineering' to an increasingly volatile and chaotic business environment, may create the comforting illusion of certainty, control and equilibrium, but the price will be paid in terms of deep robust organisational stability. You cannot buy someone else's change, you must learn how to grow your own. In the long run, we believe that this archaic brand of consulting will tend to provoke unproductive havoc and human anguish, unnecessarily. We will say more about this soon, but the message is becoming clear. Don't allow machine minded 'change' consultants to enter your company preaching certainty.

2

Intellectual Poison: How to Resist Change Perfectly

This chapter describes the main assumptions of conventional change methods, such as Business Process Reengineering (BPR) and Total Quality Management (TQM). It also indicates why these and other models do not fit current organisational reality.

We believe that the following management fads, like TQM, Downsizing, Rightsizing, Flattening, Delayering, Restructuring, Reengineering, Business Process Redesign, Mission Statements, Empowerment, and Pay-For-Performance, probably do more damage than good in the long term because their core assumptions and operating logic have a limited view of reality. To think of a modern organisation as a machine is, in our view, about as sensible as trying to use magnetic lodestone to attract a wayward spouse back home. This common practice of the middle ages, is actually just another form of magic.

Why have more than 75% of all TQM or BPR projects in the world failed?After decades of continuous success based on 'bigger is better', business went sour at the end of the 80s, and companies were forced to change. Their initial reflex was to do what they had always done: grow and centralize in good times, shrink and spin-off in bad ones. As both reflexes were based on traditional assumptions, which had worked in the past, the poor performance results produced a whole new set of problems. According to Hamel & Prahalad,

'The foundations of past success were shaken and fractured when, in all too many cases, the industrial terrain changed shape faster than top management could refashion its basic beliefs and assumptions about which markets to serve, which technologies to master, which customers to serve, and how to get the best out of employees.'[a]

The characteristic methods employed to try to transform business organisations included downsizing, process redesign, employee empowerment, overhead reduction, and portfolio rationalisation. In this way, organisations hope to quickly increase efficiency and productivity. Here are some figures:

Name Company	Announced Layoffs	Restructuring Costs (x million $)
3M	4,500	500
Black & Decker Corp.	3,000	300
Citigroup	10,400	900
Federal-Mogul Corp.	4,200	205
IBM	--	800
Johnson & Johnson	4,100	800
Lear Corp.	2,800	133
Philip Morris	2,500	630
Polaroid Corp.	2,500	300
Singer Co.	5,968	186
Stanley Works	4,500	240
Sunbeam Corp.	6,000	300
United Healthcare	1,700	700

Source: CNN-FN

---

[a] Hamel, G., and Prahalad, C.K., 1994, *Competing for the Future*, Harvard Business School Press, Boston

Lean management

In general, the only purpose of lean-management is cost reduction. This is very dangerous in times of change. Often management does not realize when to stop restructuring. They may accidentally hollow out the organisation, which is then too weak and enfeebled to adapt and compete. A few years ago *Management Today* featured a number of articles on downsizing. They argued that:

> '...the attention on cost is bound to continue. If a firm is earning 5% on 1 billion sales, then cutting costs by 1% can raise profits by as much as 19%' Why would anyone, with his eyes pointed on the next quarter's earnings, want to take the career risk to try to create the same level of return, with a growth strategy?'

Teams from Bath and Warwick University conducted an extensive analysis into lean systems for the British Institute of Personnel and Development (IPD). They concluded that:

> '...attempts to develop leaner management systems by de-layering, downsizing, business process re-engineering (BPR) and total quality management (TQM) frequently fail(ed) to live up to expectations.'[a]

Well over half of UK companies have, or are about to undergo restructuring, with most opting for downsizing, either by de-layering, offering early retirement or making redundancies. Over two-thirds of the UK's 500 largest companies have introduced TQM. Still, a survey of 880 UK managers found that only 8% believed TQM to be successful. The IPD concluded:

> 'Lean systems are far from fulfilling the promises of enhanced competitiveness and business success made by many of their advocates.'

---

[a] Institute of Personnel and Development, 9 October 1996, News Release: "Without Staff Support Lean Management May Do More Harm Than Good".

Downsizing

Downsizing promises: reducing operating costs, eliminating unneeded management tiers resulting in enhanced communication, increasing responsiveness to customers, faster decision making, employee involvement, mastering product development, streamlining corporate operations, and global competitiveness.

The following terminology, collected by De Meuse, Vanderheiden, and Bergmann, was used by companies around the year of announced layoffs. Their sample included some Fortune Top 100 firms. It tracked lay-off announcements, employment levels, and financial performance.

Company Annual Report Statement & Translation in Layoffs

Sears	'Our dramatic downsizing certainly attracted a lot of attention over the last 18 months.'	50,000
IBM	'Shortly after I (CEO Louis Gerstner) joined the company, I set as my highest priority to right-size the company as quickly as we could.'	35,000
Boeing	'Boeing continues to take the steps necessary to adjust to the market downturn.'	28,000
Kodak	'The fundamentals show that we are making real progress in reducing our cost base.'	12,000
GE	'(Our) plan includes explicit programs that will result in the closing, downsizing and streamlining of certain production, service and administrative facilities world-wide.'	10,000

Table adapted from: Bumstead, April 1994. You're Downsized!, Time, Vol. 143, No. 16, p. 22.[a]

In the United States, more than 7 million permanent layoffs have been announced since 1987. Especially the first half of 1990 was

---

[a] We listed these companies only to indicate the numbers of lay-offs. We don't believe downsizing pays off in the long run. Some of these companies are successful due to other Change practices. We will present examples from GE, Boeing, Kodak and 3M further on.

brutal.'*At a peak in 1993 the biggest US companies laid off 600,000 workers, 25% more than in 1992 (!).*'[a] CEO's such as IBM's Akers and GM's Stempel became casualties as shareholders demanded ever faster action. Lay-offs continued into early 1996, with an extra 250,000 lost in the first 6 months. Outplacement firms mushroomed! In 3 years time their number grew 35%.'*Over 1996 as a whole, Fortune 500 companies grew in revenue only 0.5% but squeezed profits up by 25.1%.*'[b]

In the UK, a similar scenario emerged from about 1989. Privatised utilities and telecoms alone lost over 100,000 people in 5 years. In addition to what's been said so far, there are more arguments against down-sizing: corporate performance shows no significant improvement, profits decrease, dividend growth is slow, product quality and productivity decrease, employee workload increases, additional stress results in higher health care expenses, low morale and job dissatisfaction result in high tardiness, absenteeism, and high turnover, stock prices can tumble if traders perceive the company as being in trouble.

In the United States between two-thirds to three-fourths of all downsizings are unsuccessful from the start. Doing-more-with-less is a naive solution. Among other things, it results in serious loss of employee loyalty. For decades we hear top executives say 'People are our greatest assets'. But when we look at what they really do with their human resources, one is left with a different conclusion. It's a different walk to all the talk. Instead of assets to develop, many managers still regard employees as costs, to be cut. This behaviour actually reveals a profound difference in character and values, between real Leaders and Managers.

---

[a] Dopson, S., Keith Ruddle and Rosemary Stewart. "Survey-Mastering Global Business: From Downsizing to Revitalisation", *Financial Times* 27/2/1998.
[b] idem

Reengineering

Reengineering aims to redesign work processes, to promote 'a fundamental rethinking and radical redesign of business processes to achieve dramatic improvements in critical, contemporary measures of performance, such as cost, quality, service and speed'.[a]

The question is 'who' is supposed to do this? The fundamental flaw in the logic of reengineering lies in its assumption of an externally imposed design approach. This is like trying to predict what will happen on an automobile drive on the motorway. It may be well intentioned, but in practice, it's often a waste of money, time and energy. Trying to predict, plan and control a real organisational change, which is so elusive, paradoxically complex, and subject to irreversible luck, by wealding an old mechanical formula that doesn't work, resembles the bizarre act of desperation that it often is. Unless the spontaneous unmanageable aspects of change are also incorporated into the otherwise useful aspects of reengineering, this fad will also have to be 'let go of'.

Reengineering, like restructuring attempts to reduce complexity, and middle management is often sacrificed. The reengineering knife hacks away not only fat, but also brain tissue! Grint and Willcocks found that 59 % of UK organisations reported BPR in 1995. Evidence indicates that BPR often fails to deliver improved organisational performance. Even its inventors, Hammer and Champy, agreed that between 50-70 % of reengineering initiatives failed to achieve their aims.

---

[a] Hammer, M., and Champy, J., 1995. *Reengineering the Corporation: A Manifesto for Business Revolution.* Nicholas Brealey Publishing, London, p32

Empowerment

Empowerment is recognising the talent and knowledge that your people already have, and allowing that to be liberated and released into the organisation. Empowerment has two crucial components[a]: The first one is trust. Trust is a value, not a cost. Lack of trust is the hidden obstacle for empowerment. Trust has to flow from top to bottom and vice versa. Employees feel vulnerable when people with more power stand above, and apart from them. This feeds distrust. Being trusted also implies that other people believe that you are responsible and capable enough to do the things that you've agreed to do.

The second component of empowerment involves the sharing of sensitive information across departmental boundaries. Autonomous employees need an open free culture and an 'open book' management style. Empowerment can be encouraged through a reward system that recognises entrepreneurship and customer appreciation. Also, giving special training on demand and granting stock or profit incentives gives people the motivation and knowledge to acquire full business and IT literacy.

The Learning Organisation

According to Peter Senge, the learning organisation is a *'community of commitment'*[b], in which all members of the organisation are dedicated to meaningful lives and work. They continually learn together how to create and realise their dreams and how to continuously remain open to change. In practice, maximum learning happens around difficulties and handling failure. Overcoming failure, along with creative disciplined

---

[a] Randolph, W. A., 1995. "Navigating the Journey to Empowerment", *Organisational Dynamics*. Spring, 4, pp19-32

[b] Kofman, and Senge, P.M., 1993. "Communities of Commitment: The Heart of Learning Organisations", *Organisational Dynamics*, Vol. 22, No. 2, pp5-23

persistence, is what permits success.

The complete business cycle involves four steps; you make, sell, bill and collect. Business literate entrepreneurship means people taking an interest in all four processes. This combines the economic roles of inventor, producer, seller and counter. It may also include being a consumer too.

These four functions got separated in the Western methods of organisation, a couple of hundred years ago. To control the information complexity, they became departmentalised. Total business and performance commitment will flow from a complete revision of the assumptions which underpin this fragmented scientificconcept of work. Modern information technology makes it possible to restore the complete business perspective to working people, and to redefine roles and responsibilities in ways which put them back together. This builds motivation, commitment and loyalty among employees. That's one reason why firms like GE and Microsoft include stock options and profit bonuses in many of their people's reward packages. The need for external control diminishes when each person can be trusted to behave like a fractal section of the whole business.

In order for a whole ation to be able to learn, power and information need to be redistributed among everyone, instead of remaining solely in the hands of the managers. Most senior executives fully realise in theory, that business leaders must democratise from the top, before they can expect participation to emerge and grow from the bottom.

Desire for change and fundamental learning are two implicit cornerstones in any well managed change programme. We believe that most people want to succeed. Letting the real market forces into a firm, so that people can individually see and feel the whole reality, will spontaneously start the change.

The need to control the complex environment

'...implementation always depends on relinquishing some control, so that people on the job can feel the satisfaction of turning chaos into order – each person in his or her own way.' [a]

Art Kliener, MIT Centre For Organisational Learning

In general we can differentiate three specific manifestations of our need to control the environment. They are: competition, fragmentation and reactivity. Each represents a system of thought which grew out of various scientific, religious, and philosophical roots, to appear in European, and subsequently American, business practices, particularly over the last three centuries.

The first manifestation of a control need is competition. You only compete when something is considered to be scarce, not abundant. Abundance let's everyone win.

It is perhaps no mere coincidence that, according to Dr. Richard Leakey, the history of organised warfare began with the start of farming, about 10,000 years ago. Agriculture had a profound and deeply transforming social outcome, because it bred a sense of ownership and not stewardship, of the Earth and its creatures. Farming seeks to dominate Nature.

Let's examine the deeper issues closely. First, ownership gives people something to defend, or to envy. Second, once you can control and dominate Nature, the next step is to start doing it to each other. Third, agriculture enabled a few people to amass the very unequal resources of power and wealth with which to do this. Modern day nomads like the Aborigines of Australia have a 40,000 year old culture of cooperation with Nature, and with each other, not a culture of domination. Land 'ownership' was also a very alien idea to the natives of North America. When seen in this context, the modern age of information dwarfs the 18th century

---

[a] in a letter to the editor, *Harvard Business Review*, Jan/Feb 1997, p164

Industrial Revolution and even the Agricultural Revolution, in terms of its fundamental social, political and economic potential for global change. Information technology across the whole planet is a truly massive scale media extension.

In business, we can already see that global information and the capability of communication to share, is having just such a profound transformational effect on people and organisation. The internet has become the world's storehouse of knowledge and is set to become the major commercial highway. The old paradigm is shifting, and the seeds of a new critical mass of socially aware consumers are now becoming visible.

Officially, in many Western firms, strategy is still measured by the competitive advantage which it may ultimately confer. Long-term symbiosis and associations which produce sharevalue and excellence, still remains subservient to profit and dividends. Consequently, quality, price, and service are all translated into terms of profit margin and bottom line results. It's a pure money value competition, scored in numbers. A characteristic of such a competition is that it gives first priority to instruments and technical systems. Things must come before people, because that's how the results are measured. In other words, costs, revenues and capital assets are priorities. In such a social context of scarcity, this means that there is very limited attention left, for people. Hiring and firing people depends on the demands of the technology, rather than the other way around. This view seriously ignores the changes happening among the buying public of the world and the human intellectual capital assets of the information age.

Another problem with competition is that it creates false imperatives for managers and their careers. Often, in intensely competitive organisations, it is publically more important that strategy looks good, rather than that it works. Also, the existence of competition itself is rarely questioned. External competition is assumed to be natural and good, and the existence of any internal competition is officially denied by the top 'teamplayers'. These dangerous assumptions often result in quick fix solutions, which only focus on fast, visual, and measurable short term career results. The consequences and responsibility for what happens in the long term simply gets passed on as a legacy for future colleagues to sort out. Profit competition doesn't generate or move product, only enthusiasm does. Enthusiasm and knowledge of the customer must join with similar enthusiasm for the product, inside the firm. Peter Senge showed how competitive assumptions among auto executives, about 'why people buy cars' wrecked the US car industry, 'The once proud (American) auto industry has suffered ... In 1950, America had 76 percent of the world's motor vehicle production. In 1995, our share had fallen to 25 percent.'[a]

'Competitive situations...tend to be less efficient and result in poorer quality products...the minute people need anything at all from the efforts of others, or share a future fate, cooperation has all the advantages. This finding has been known since Peter Blau's studies in the 1950's.'[b]

Rosabeth Moss Kanter

Some typical street-level assumptions about competition are that it improves performance and learning abilities, and also that it stimulates the search for innovation and invention.

In reality however, competition produces secrecy and the hoarding of critical information, plus the bad general habit of focusing on one's own needs rather than the organisation's, or worse, the customer's. Competition creates and feeds off problems, not solutions. Good collective solutions are often invisible to a competitive mind-set. The old rule here is simply to win, often at the expense of openness, trust, and co-operation inside the company. Irresponsible individual behaviour destroys collective learning and a group's ability to self-organise.

Information technology requires a modern organisational

---

[a] Tetenbaum, T. J., 1998. "Shifting Paradigms: From Newton to Chaos", *Organisational Dynamics*. Spring, pp21-32
[b] Rosabeth Moss Kanter, *When Giants Learn To Dance*, Touchstone-Simon & Schuster, 1986, p75

culture to make it work. People who are fixed on competitive win/lose values and behaviour are avoided. Competition is about taking, but cooperation is about giving. In an organisation which is fit for the information age, a few rules of personal conduct apply. These are:

- Admit your mistakes, to fix things fast!
- Don't need to be right. If you can't get win/win, walk away.
- Join up and work where you are welcome most.
- Go to your next business meeting to give. Don't ask anyone for anything.
- Look for solutions that emerge naturally, by working together.
- Help your associates to become successful and to realize their own dreams.

A system at war with itself cannot survive for long. A modern study of the process of evolution, must then also include symbiosis and cooperation, as well as competition. The recent micro-biological studies of Dr. L. Margulis and others, show that it is a combination of both symbiosis and competition which allows plants, animals and humans, to survive and reproduce. The 19th century interpretation of the survival of the fittest 'individual' is wrong. Darwin actually wrote about the survival of the fittest 'population'. Evolution as a process, as Darwin understood it works across populations, not individuals.

'One may say that there is a force like a hundred thousand wedges trying to force every kind of adapted structure into the gaps in the economy of nature, or rather forming gaps by thrusting out weaker ones.'
Charles Robert Darwin, Notebook on Transmutation of Species, 1837

You, as an individual do not evolve, except into your own children. Evolution is a holistic process which favours, or condemns, the next generation, not the present one. A population of animals or humans survives, by genetically and phenotypically (teaching and learning) transmitting a combined adaptive advantage, not by a single member's efforts. It must not be forgotten that cooperative social behaviour has evolved because it confers some collective advantage for a species, in its environment. Altruism and self sacrifice is commonly found among all social animals, that's what keeps a species together.

The biological definition of a species hangs on the compatability between members to reproduce fertile offspring. Clearly, the entire human race is biologically one species and we can now inter-act and communicate mentally, emotionally and spiritually across the whole world. This is the first time it's ever happened on such a scale. Physical barriers of time, space and empathic understanding have all suddenly vanished. It was satellite television that brought down the Berlin wall, not guns. And, just like a snowflake evolves, this remarkable change grew from the inside-out. Today, the signals for business are clear. Well informed global village citizens prefer to associate with decent business firms, that know how to network and cooperate, especially with the environment. Business Ethics is no longer a boardroom lawyer's joke.

Informed people will see to it that their world is not run by criminals. The blind dogma of compete at all costs creates suffering, loss and damage. It also destroys diversity. Seen in a modern ecological context, irresponsible commercial exploitation and greed cannot be allowed to persist. Industrial pollution, environmental desecration and over-population is eliminating so much of our planet's essential living diversity, that we are now entering what is becoming known among bio-paleontologists as the Sixth Extinction.

The Sixth Extinction

According to the fossil record, there have been five cataclysmic events in the evolutionary history of life on this planet. Each event reduced the variety of all living diversity very significantly. The last extinction of this magnitude, the Cretaceous catastrophy, occurred 65 million years ago when a large high velocity asteroid smashed into the Earth. The impact was so violent, that the dust rising from it blacked out the Sun and the whole Earth cooled. This event lead to the extinction of many diverse species and is believed to have wiped out most of the Dinosaurs. The sixth extinction is well underway, and we humans are both its cause and possible remedy. That's the scale of the legacy that we are going to leave behind for our children if we cannot change our competitive behaviour and collectively prevent the sixth extinction. Nature cannot think. Evolution only makes conscious decisions through us. Politics is about the way people in organisations behave, not what they say. No decent business person can afford to ignore the ethics of ecology today, and the global buying public is increasingly aware of it.

'We learn to break the world apart and disconnect ourselves from it ...' [a]

The second manifestation of the need to control, is fragmentation. A typical old science response to a complex problem is to deal purely rationally and analytically with it.

See the problem as a thing; an object; independent of the people who are responsible for it. Cut the problem into pieces. Examine these pieces and then cobble the bits back together, to supposedly represent and function as a whole again. Complex problems are not objects, which you can slice up. Rather, a 'problem' is just a name used by people to describe a holistic

---

[a] Capra, F., 1984. *Het Keerpunt: wetenschap, samenleving en de toekomst van de nieuwe cultuur.* (The Turning Point) Uitgeverij Contact; Amsterdam.

inter-dependant set of issues and activities, which they wish to change. You have to involve those people who are close enough to the action and who see the situation as a 'problem', because they will also probably know what to do, best. Get them looking for solutions, not problems. Tell your people not to come to you with problems. Ask them to bring their likely solutions and you will help them to choose what to do next.

> *'Work division is the foundation of organisation; indeed the reason for organisation.'* [a]
> Luther Gulick & Lyndall Urwick

Fragmentation not only leads to hierarchy, it has also made us feel dependent on what we might call experts', or specialists'. Many consultants make their living from 'fixing' other people's problems in this way. One unfortunate result is that the people who originally perceived something as a problem do not get the chance to learn. When the consultant leaves the organisation, the people along with their root ignorance of the problem, remains.

> *'We're going to have to figure out how to organise people in ways that enable them to coordinate their activities without wasteful and intrusive systems of control and without too much predefinition of what a job is.'* [b]
> Robert B. Shapiro, CEO Monsanto

Another outcome of fragmentation is the separation of work into many departments. Departments work independently, with walls around them. People in fragmented departments do not know, nor do they usually care much, about what people in other departments, or even what customers want. 'That isn't in the job description'. Often a company's problem is not about finding the right person for the job, but rather thinking in terms of jobs at all.

---

[a] Luther Gulick & Lyndall Urwick, "Papers On The Science of Administration", New York Institute of Public Administration, 1937, p3
[b] Jean Magretta, "Growth Through Global Sustainability", *Harvard Business Review*, Jan/Feb 1997, p87

Breaking down the mental and physical walls between jobs and departments can't be effectively commanded from above. It can sometimes happen in a crisis, or when something new needs to be done so urgently that a few brave souls start working together.

Job, literally means either a piece of work, or a measured section of time. The word appeared in the 16th century. The concept of a job is already a fragmentation. As William Bridges wrote :

> 'The job is a social artefact, although it is so deeply embedded in our consciousness that most of us have forgotten its artificiality or the fact that most societies since the beginning of time have done just fine without jobs. The job concept emerged early in the nineteenth century to package the work that needed doing in the growing factories and bureaucracies of the industrialising nations.'[a]

We will explore this more when we discuss the mental shift from thinking like an employee, to thinking like an entrepreneur.

The third manifestation of our need to control the complex environment, is reactivity. Normally companies start restructuring only after they have diagnosed an crisis. It seems like the only real motivation for seeking deep change. Also the attitude of managers is strongly driven by events. They run from one problem to the next. Lean, mean and agile is the buzzword. Cutting out anything resembling slack, and thus reducing organisational flexibility, is the reality. In such a situation, people usually react to periods of crises, by working longer hours. Reacting to a crisis can produce change, but a constant diet of crisis can eventually traumatise people. Crises provide very little learning and only deliver short-term expedient results. Reactivity brings organisations into an orbit of, crisis --> change --> one time solution --> waiting --> next crisis.

To assist organisations to climb out of that particular orbit,

---

[a] Bridges, W., 1994. *Jobshift: How To Prosper in a Workplace Without Jobs*, 1st edition. Addison-Wesley Publishing Company, Reading.

Professor Chris Argyris distinguishes between single-loop and double-loop learning. Most companies only know single-loop learning. For example, top management yells 'let's introduce SAP, because we need to service customers faster!'. Their unspoken assumptions are:

1. What we do, is right,
2. We need to do it faster, better, cheaper,
3. SAP works for other firms,
4. We are not different from other firms,
5. It'll work for us.

This diagnostic thinking is single-loop. They can only learn to improve an existing habit. With double-loop learning, those same managers would question their own assumptions, and ask themselves:

1. Do we do the right things?
2. Do we need the speed?,
3. Does SAP work?,
4. Are we in fact similar to others?

Conclusion

'This is about us. What do we want to do? Companies aren't machines anymore. We have thousands of independent agents trying to self-coordinate because it is in their interests to do so...people only give to people...They care intensely about it, and they organise themselves to do it...I don't mean to romanticise it, but, bye and large, self-regulating systems are probably going to be more productive than those based primarily on control loops...' [a]

Robert B. Shapiro, CEO Monsanto

You must grow your own change. In the elephant's graveyard of the Fortune 500, lie the bones of thousands of failed change management programmes. Most were bought from outside consultants, as expensive universal package systems which looked good on paper, didn't work in practice and were eventually discarded. Many of these lethal implants actually killed their hosts. This is not suprising as they were designed and built on scientific illusions of certainty, from an archaic form of deterministic logic which can only work successfully under historically stable business conditions. These programmes were actually built to control and manage the past. They fail in the 'here and now' because they harbour some very unscientific assumptions about how to deal with a complex chaotic new business environment. They also fail to understand the dramatic roles of open information, purpose, commitment, creativeness and our natural human ability to self-organise.

It may be of academic interest to try to engineer a universal mechanical model of the ideal human organisation as if it were some kind of isolated object, and then attempt to measure how reality differs from this. It is however neurotic to blame that chaotic reality, for not permitting the idealized system to work in practice. Personally speaking, we wouldn't fight reality. Chaos is

---

[a] ibid, pp85-87

the one fact of modern business life which needs greater executive understanding. In the following sections we will present a more chaos literate approach to change management.

Part 2

LOVE CHANGE (AS MUCH AS YOU USED TO HATE IT)

In this section we introduce you to some of the major issues involved in transforming a traditional organisation. What can replace conventional planning, strategic determinism, division of labor, boss-focused control & command, top-down hierarchy, and parts and departments? We explore the concept of self-organising units, in a business organisation which is shaped by the reality of customers; staffed by people who freely work together in teams as inter-dependant entrepreneurs, and who think and act like suppliers.

'Top down...or bottom up exercises...don't sound like helpful concepts to me...There is no top or bottom. That's just a metaphor ...' [a]

Robert B. Shapiro

We discard low trust notions of top down division and control, and start to think more holistically about how to:

- *connect all people to market reality and complete information,*
- *liberate emotional and creative energy,*
- *improve the chances of luck and opportunistic accidents,*
- *recognize, welcome and develop fresh opportunity.*

---

[a] ibid, p85

- *combine productive relationships,*
- *nurture individual excellence and total customer commitment,*

Once we can facilitate these activities as leaders in our own organisational units, we can start to think about organising entrepreneurs for innovation and high performance, on a large scale. In such an enterprise, continuously exploring possibility then becomes the prime organisational purpose. When this is done well, the business results automatically follow. In the first chapter we describe the four essential Paradigm Shifts. In the second chapter we present the essential differences between Evolution and Revolution as Strategies of Change.

1

The Four Paradigm Shifts

We are about to describe a holistic non-linear view of organisation. It is impossible for us to specifically prescribe what you should do, or stop doing, first. Deeper into the text, you will learn by yourself, how to grow your own change.To facilitate your sequential reading and comprehension of this chapter/section, we have clustered the main issues, under the banner headlines of 'The 1st, 2nd, 3rd, & 4th Shift'. This does not necessarily indicate any cause-effect relationship or a particular linear step-sequence.

This method of writing is inspired by Eastern Process-Thinking. We were introduced to this way of presenting information by Professor Sigmund Kvaloy of Norway, who is very accomplished in both Ecological and Process Philosophy. The geometrical metaphor for the method is the spiral. In the first circular spin, the reader is introduced to the relevant concepts, haphazardly. The next twist repeats and connects the concepts to go deeper. This process continues until an implicit 'vision tranfer' occurs, as both the writer and the reader, begin to reach a similar cognitive understanding.

The method allows the reader the time to reflect and think deeply, rather than to immediately accept or reject the information, which is the conventional model of Western epistemology. As any traveller to Japan will know, the process thinking approach is also typical for Tokyo cab-drivers. Clients first vaguely describe the direction that they want to go, e.g. East Tokyo. Then they add more precision as the journey unfolds, e.g. in the vicinity of the Sony building. They finally conclude with the 'Ban Sen Juku Restaurant'.

We start by briefly discussing the budget which may be

necessary for change. We also reframe the question of change resistance from a customer/competitor point of view. Essentially in 'The 1st Shift' we focus on the customer as the principle guide for change; on what motivates people to work, and the search for the simplest way to change. In 'The 2nd Shift', we describe the change in mind-set as people stop seeing themselves as employees, and start to imagine themselves behaving and feeling like entrepreneurs. Such imagination inspires and guides energy. We also mention the powerful effect of individual values on people's behavior and personal decision making heuristics (models). Values[a], compared to vision, have received little attention in management literature.

In 'The 3rd Shift' we present some aspect of chaos theory as interesting new metaphors for business. We introduce concepts like attractors, the cycles of control and chaos, spontaneous self-organisation and sensitivity to initial conditions. We also begin to explain how to educate entrepreneurship.

In 'The 4th Shift' we discuss the importance of trust and open critical feedback, particularly 'upline', from the weaker bottom to the more powerful top of the organisation. Feedback across the organisation promotes the necessary learning and rapid organised cooperation, which directly contributes to the speed of change. Many of the concepts introduced in this section will in turn be expanded upon later, to eventually be fused together into a more or less complete Change Lens.

Prepare a realistic change budget

Change is not just something to believe in, invariably you must invest in it too. Transformational change can cost money at first, because it's not about doing more of the same things better, it's

---

[a] We don't mean Ethics here, but rather what your company values and what your customers value.

about learning to do things in a completely different way. It usually takes longer to invent and learn the new ways than to forget the old.[a] Behavioral psychologists claim that it can take 18 months of repetition (reinforcement) before a new behavior becomes a natural habitual part of you. John P. Kotter, Professor of Leadership, and his team at Harvard Business School, quantified the amount of change they noticed over 7-years in what they called [one of the most successful change efforts they had seen][b]. On a scale from 1 (low) to 10 (high) they noted that the change peaked in year 5, which is 3 years after the first visible positive results emerged. Ok, it's hard to generalise, but some changes may require more confidence, patience and cash, than others.

Change-resistance is slow suicide

'Change is scary, but people volunteer for dangerous tasks only when they feel safe.'[c]

Today, working people are learning to either fear, or to hate change, especially if you call it 'change'. They have good reason for this. Many business organisations 'zap' from one blind change formula to the next, often destroying people's careers, private lives and hopes. At the time of writing, the latest miracle fad is a combination of Mergers & Acquisitions, followed by downsizing, recentralization into centralised 'service' centers, and finally get some new technology – SAP is a favorite – and hire a firm of consultants to glue it all together. Even Panoramix[d], the famous Druid in the Comic-book Astérix, would be jealous of such a 'magical potion'!

---

[a] Yoshinori Yokoyama, *McKinsey Quarterly* 4 (1992), pp116-27
[b] Kotter, John P. "Leading Change: Why Transformation Efforts Fail", *Harvard Business Review* March-April 1995
[c] Thomas A. Stewart, "Managing Change–How to Lead a Corporate Revolution", *Fortune* 28/11/94, p27
[d] "Getafix" in the English editions

One US giant – let's call them A – recently purchased B (turnover: $1.3 billion, profit: $150 million), for twice the stock-market value. A also paid B's debts ($700 million), and estimated the integration costs at approximately $200 million. In total, A paid $3.5 billion for B. If A had taken a loan for this amount at 5% interest, it would need to pay about $180 million per year to service that loan, but in 1998 B's profits were $150 million!

A also invested $125 million in a SAP software installation. B invested $50 million for SAP in the US, and $20 million in Europe. If we assume, at the current rate of technical obsolecense, a 5 year life time for SAP, both A & B need the following annual savings to achieve a healthy internal rate of return of 15%: A $37.5 million, B $21 million. A applies the simplest way to generate quick savings, namely cutting costs by laying off 700 of B's 6000 people. They assume that fewer people will still be able to continue to produce the profit rate of $150 million. This assumption however, may be lethal for B's flexibility to be able to adapt in a robust way to any unforeseeable major external changes.

To maintain your flexibility to change effectively, it's better to start creating new positive incentives around customers, rather than trying to manipulate resistance, or to cut fat. Work on the motivation of the people you've got first. Move people into new unfamiliar groups. Then take them through the wall, before they even realise that they've got one.

Organisational transformation on any scale is about building momentum and then keeping it up. It's like spinning a wheel fast enough to fundamentally escape orbit. If you don't reach a critical momentum level in time, entropic 'change fatigue' will probably damage your organisation.

Trust begins with the owners. To get the right depth of change penetration, speed and scale, the full confidence of the major share-holders is required. As we've shown, you may have to sacrifice some cash flow, to win on longer term flexibility and share value.

Everyone in business already thinks that the customer is king. They have to start to feel it too. An attractive, well understood change programme, anchored to what your customers truly value, can promote entrepreneurship and eliminate much internal resistance naturally. A business organisation exists only to make its customers successful. This is its main operating guideline, and this is what it must be allowed to deliver superbly. A typically bureaucratic business hierarchy has, over the years, lost sight of its paymaster and forgotten its purpose. When, by habit, it serves the interests of itself first, it has become myopic; just like a sky that people only look up at, not out of. Nowadays in business, that's dangerous.

THE FIRST SHIFT: Follow the path of least resistance

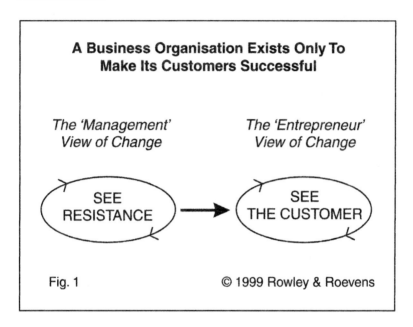

A Business Organisation Exists Only To Make Its Customers Successful

The 'Management' View of Change

The 'Entrepreneur' View of Change

SEE RESISTANCE → SEE THE CUSTOMER

Fig. 1   © 1999 Rowley & Roevens

As we indicate in the illustration, salaried managers may view change in a different way to entrepreneurs. When a typical salaried manager thinks about change, nightmare pictures of angry subordinates and possible labor union havoc may appear. His motivation to change rests at zero. Entrepreneurs and entrepreneurial managers, would keep their mind's eye on the target: the customer. They also realize that everybody must begin to understand that satisfying the customer is the only guarantee of the business' survival and for continuing profits. Everyone must grow to realize that satisfying the customer is the only income security that they have.

Make the customer the leader of the hierarchy

'Stemberg understands that having his managers spend lots of time solving customer problems sends clear signals to everyone about the organisation's priorities.' [a]

Market forces must quickly reach into and touch every person in your firm today. As Maverick Ricardo Semler of Semco, a Brazilian manufacturer of pumps, dishwashers, cooling units, mixers and even entire factories puts it:

'The pressure is also greater at Semco because we truly believe in the market. We don't protect anybody from the vicissitudes of the business cycle or the crazy Brazilian economy [with inflation sometimes running up to 900%]. This is not for everybody – certainly not for bureaucrats who spend careers digging themselves in like soldiers in the trenches.' [b]

One way to bring a hierarchy closer to a market driven association of entrepreneurs is to make the customer the head of the pyramid. The Chief Executive could set the example and symbolically replace herself, or himself, with a representative customer at the next general meeting, to show precisely who is the real boss. Once the customer is made central to the purpose of a change initiative, then the value that each person in the organisation creates for the customer, in every branch of the process, is the constant reference. Tony Hope offers some interesting insights on customers when he said that:

'Xerox launched a small revolution when it targeted to make happy customers VERY happy. A very happy customer re-orders 6 times more often than a happy one!' Moreover, Mc Kinsey& Co. calculated that 68% of customers leave a business due to careless service. This compares to a 14% departure due to product dissatisfaction, a 9%

---

[a] *Fortune* 10/7/95, p54
[b] *Maverick,*1994, p156

departure due to better prices elsewhere and a 5% farewell due to new distribution.'[a]

Hi-fi distributor Richer Sounds uses customer satisfaction to measure a sales person's bonuses. The result is that salespeople do not push the most expensive items, they listen carefully to the customer's needs and wishes. Its owner believes that this approach will lead to better sustainable profit in the long run, than a policy of one-time 'hit and run' sales.

Why do we show up here?

Change the reward and budget systems first. Then change people's roles and relationships. This promotes new rituals, symbols and language which all focus more an customer appreciation, rather than on boss appreciation. There is more to it which we'll discuss in detail later, but that's the basic idea up to now.

---

[a] Hope, Tony in "Op zoek naar rendabele klanten". (Searching for Profitable Customers). Vacature, 4/1/1997, p5

THE SECOND SHIFT: Managing the entrepreneurial spirit?

Management organisation models developed for herding sheep don't work with cats. When an organisation flock of many sheep with only one head, starts to become one large cat with many diverse heads, this raises an unfamiliar leadership challenge. A good dog can handle a flock of sheep, but how do you manage a bunch of cats? How could you possibly lead a large herd of independent pussy cats, on foot over the open fields from say, where you live, to wherever you happen to work?

Clearly, the only decent way to lead cats like this, is with enough of the right cat food, for each different cat. Entrepreneurs are motivated by their own desires and dreams. They may appreciate some individualised coaching and occasional alignment, but they definitely will not tolerate conventional management.

Entrepreneurs have a similar psychological profile to customers

The profiles of both Entrepreneurs and Customers are based on free and open choice. They require a supportive organisation which is dedicated to help them individually to succeed. Entrepreneurs by definition are autonomous, and selectively demand transparent leadership. They unite in hope, and only trust in leaders whose values exemplify those same standards that they have set for themselves and to which they can truly and passionately own.

Entrepreneurs are growing. Harvard Business School Professor John Kotter argues that 40% of the 1974 graduates are entrepreneurs. Details can be found in his book. *The New Rules: How to Succeed In Today's Post-Corporate World.* Harvard

Business School expects that by 2010 more than 60% of its graduates will form their own businesses. As William Sahlman, the school's professor of entrepreneurial finance, puts it:

'The best and the brightest, who used to be attracted to consulting and investment banking, are now saying, I want to be my own boss.'[a]

In the UK, Cranfield Mananagement School offers the entrepreneurial'Business Growth Programme'. When Cranfield researchers followed up on the programme's graduates some years later, they found that their companies had grown 4 times faster than those of non-participating entrepreneurs.[b] In addition, many employees will be forced to think and act as entrepreneurs because of external pressures. Johan Stekelenburg, former chairman of FNV, Holland's largest labor union, said something atypical for a union chief, namely that the future of work, would be a full-time contract at an employment agency. Stekelenburg realizes that people will be hired and fired more flexibly. The FNV therefore emphasizes continuous education and decent contracts, so flex-workers will have stronger bargaining powers.

In times of chaos, values come before vision

The quality of a leader is quickly known among the followers and this requires a tall order of character and strength. It also naturally points to the eventual democratic election of future business leaders by the followers, not the owners. In an open flexible organisation, nothing is hidden and there's nowhere to hide. Visible action speaks louder than words. In rapidly growing industries, or in the wildly fluctuating economies of some

---

[a] Lord, Mary & R.G. Westfall. "Running their own show" *US News & World Report 1997*
[b] Quacquarelli, N. and S. McIntosh. "Entrepreneurial MBAs around the world". *The MBA Career Guide*, Fall 1996, p19

countries, uncertainty quickly replaces any rules.

Where major environmental changes happen continuously and unpredictably, the fastest response time comes once internal values govern and guide everyone's behaviour. This simply means doing the right things at the right time, for the right reasons. What a business culture truly values and rewards in day to day action is therefore a hot, continuous live issue. Remember, what we are now describing is a professional association of entrepreneurs, not an army of employees. Entrepreneurs tend to follow their own visions best. Unless a vision is naturally attractive and resonant to associates, it will surely breed cynicism, alienation or contempt. Henry Ford's original vision was *'to create a car that the working man can afford'*. His own working men understood and felt that dream just as well as his customers did, and that's one key to effective visioning. Vision becomes powerful in a business organisation, when it strikes a chord of harmony between those things that your people value, and those that customers also value. In the customer hierarchy market, customer value always comes first. From this, real vision can emerge.

THE THIRD SHIFT: Chaos as a competitive resource

'The NT project ran 'right on the edge of chaos.' [a]

Lou Perazzoli, Senior NT Executive, Microsoft

In this section we introduce some elements of chaos theory into business organisation. We discuss attractors, the cycles of control and chaos, self-organisation, and sensitivity to initial conditions. We also examine how to educate entrepreneurship.

Discipline without control

'...Attractors aught to be very reassuring...chaos in a chaotic attractor is very bounded and the degree to which things go haywire is extremely limited.' [b]

How do we understand Attractors? First, Attractors are not magnetic; they are outcomes without identifiable, specific causes. Attractors just happen and manifest themselves as recognisable patterns which repeat as similar, but are never the same.

Floris Takens and David Ruelle chose the 'Attractor' concept to describe the paterned outcome of a powerful invisible locus. Regular Attractors describe the behaviour of simple periodic systems like the gravitational orbit of the planets. Chaotic or 'Strange' Attractors describe the non-random behaviour of complex dynamic systems like clouds, epidemics, traffic, and human organisations.

Points moving around a Chaotic Attractor will appear somewhere on it, but one can't predict where or when they will turn up. Unlike random disorder, these points don't fly off into

---

[a] W.C.Taylor, "Control In An Age Of Chaos", *Harvard Business Review* (Nov/Dec 1994), p74
[b] Rudy Rucker, Op.cit.

infinity, but turn at the boundary (of maximum separation), and then head back towards the core. Human beings are equipped to live in a chaotic universe; we can recognize and interpret the patterns in a system's behavior. Thus the farmer knows when to sow by watching the weather, and the car driver knows when to indicate and merge into the self-organising chaos of the freeway.

Any modern supermarket depends on the self-organising behaviour of the passing shopper. Many regular customers, are first Attracted by the 'one stop' convenience, bulk savings, or location of the store. Once inside, they oscillate chaotically' around highlighted aspects of each product's value (e.g. Price, Quality, Consistency, Availability, Seasonality, etc.). Unlike the old corner shop, the supermarket sets the shopper free in time and space to explore, and to self-select. It also allows any prospective buyer to touch, inspect, and physically capture the goods. Essentially, it runs itself efficiently and at low cost, because of formal under-management and cultural business values which in addition to sound measured 'shrinkage' or theft, are based on large scale trust. The supermarket owners don't impose much intrusive control on people, instead, they have learned to understand and trust the self-organising behaviour of the typical honest shopper as they gravitate towards what each individual finds attractive. Surfing on the internet is another example of self-organising chaotic attractor behaviour. People naturally move towards what they may like and simultaneously try to avoid what they imagine they don't like.

A freely self-organising business unit could package and present what its own customers value to its own associates in much the same way. Natural Attractor-Motivation is based on the psychology of desire and choice, not on the psychology of need. We will discuss this important difference later, because Attractor-Motivation can spontaneously generate and liberate high quality individual commitment and customer loyalty among your associates, and vice versa.

Whatever attracts customers to buy your goods or services, must be clearly identified and linked in the reward system and culture, with whatever Attracts your associates to perform. It really is that simple. Once you get the reward bridge organised internally, you can safely back off and leave the culture to trust and self-organisation.

Increased customer and associate interaction can liberate and allow synergy to happen. This can mean your people creatively spotting, identifying and picking up early, on new Attractors as they spontaneously emerge. Customers meeting with associates can be a great source of both inspiration and innovation. Such windfall bounty cannot be designed or commanded, but thanks to Chaos Theory, it can now be better understood. In a successful modern business organisation, the main chaotic 'Attractors' must resonate (at a profit), to whatever the Customers value. With self-organizing systems, the purpose is not to make something happen, but to make the best opportunity for it to happen, all by itself. That's unlike following a traditional boss vision of the 'official future', for example, to be No.1 in the industry. Seeing events through a self-organizing perpective, puts that performance goal as one possible outcome, and it probably won't happen by focusing people on the numbers made by the competition.

Self-organizing behaviour?

'Self-organizing quantum systems thrive on ambiguity. They are...delicately poised between order and chaos....Too static, it runs down...too chaotic, it breaks apart. It needs a creative balance of chaos and order to thrive.' [a]

Planning is a limited and often misleading tool where change is involved. Navigating the unknown requires an internal compass of values, not a map. The rules are few. Individually or in groups, people must combine disciplined high energy with rapid organized co-operation, in order to deal effectively and fast with uncertainty

---

[a] D. Zohar & I. Marshall, *The Quantum Society*, Flamingo, 1994:122

and change. Just like sports athletes or a top film crew, such purposeful motivation comes from an emotional dedication to their personal reputation, the lure of the project, and often commitment to each other. It is well known in the military that most professional soldiers do not continue to risk their lives to fight for their country, for freedom, for democracy, for the Queen, or for any other principle. Soldiers fight because they are afraid and for their buddies; their team-members.

World class excellence demands self-organizing teams of highly disciplined natural talent relentlessly targeting specific challenges which, for internal, personal reasons, attract and excite them. Fully committed teams select their own challenges and talent best. According to Psychologist Brian Tracy, talent means doing what you're good at, and you don't remember learning it. For an excellent description of team alignment we invite you to read Peter Senge's *The Fifth Discipline: The Art & Practice of the Learning Organisation.*

Educating entrepreneurship

Learning to become your own toughest boss means that you train yourself to become your own best paid employee. As a new culture and climate of trust replaces contract and control, Personnel professionals and change leaders can play a vital new coaching role. They must paradoxically facilitate and run new projects, which enable people to learn how to resourcefully self-direct and motivate themselves through chaos and complexity. And to deliver. Just like the combat experienced sergeant told the rookie lieutenant in Vietman, 'Sir, you must shoot, move and communicate!' Some firms like Semco, Brazil, even set former employees up in business for themselves. Educating entrepreneurship creates the Network Organisation of the future.

When Hans Baranek, boss of 'Nürnberg Fuerther Fusswegreinigung', a street-cleaning company, retired, he gave his company away to Moestafa Berk, then 38, his most loyal employee. Berk had always dreamt of having his own business and told newspapers, 'I still can't believe my eyes!' First generation entrepreneurs who build up a family business require a solid dedication from the following generations. Norbert Joris of ETAP, a market leader in lighting, keeps company ownership separate from management. One of his son's-in-law, an ex-Philips executive, applied to ETAP without informing the family. When the personnel manager invited him for an interview, the manager told him he 'had to ask his father-in-law'!

Rotary Clubs from India and Canada offered two-day classes in entrepreneurship to 400 out of more than 100,000 Bombay street-children. The kids learned sales techniques, how to make incense sticks, how to set up a flower or a food stall, and even how to bribe government officials. This is necessary because since 1978 the government refuses to administer any new licenses for street merchants. Life on the streets of Bombay is brutal: every month about 5 kids attempt suicide, 3/4s use drugs like hasj and 'brown sugar', a kind of heroin, and all are at the mercy of the police. 17-year old Vikki, an entrepreneurship graduate, received a $4.5 loan to set up his business: toast with a vegetable spread at 15 cents a piece. At the end of the day he makes a $4 profit, while typical street-children only make $2.

Network organisations create size without mass

'Organisation charts lag what's happening....And a lot of people can't figure out how to draw it any other way.' [a]

Douglas Smith

Unlike a traditional structure which pre-defines role authority and fixed reporting relationships, a Network Organisation accepts the

---

[a] John A. Byrne, "The Horizontal Corporation", *Business Week*, 20/12/93, p49

'Phantom Power' of temporary unofficial authority, as normal. It encourages people to move and mix freely. People must simply do whatever must be done.

How can we spot change leaders? John R. Katzenbach, author of *Real Change Leaders*, describes them as 'focused, determined, willing to break rules, and great at motivating their troops.'[a]. Katzenbach suggests that for large-scale change you need about 1/3 of your middle managers as change leaders. The age range seems to be 25-40, and 1/3 are women.

If business leaders need to know where people are, or, what they are doing, they can replace Organisation Charts (describing what should happen), with Sociograms describing what just happened. We have created a tool for this, called the Network Tracker. Contact us at r.rowley@glo.be or jr385@cornell.edu for further information.

In some geriatric hospitals patients receive a bracelet with a computer radio-chip. This allows one single nurse to track and monitor the movements of several hundred patients, who are all free to wander around as they please. Such a system could also be applied in a high trust business organisation for fun, just to show the exact communication channels that people really use. The whole organisation network could even be shown live, in real time, on a large screen. This would be a great way to liberate corporate identity. Of course, it requires integrity and acceptance. But it's much quicker and more immediate, to monitor the actual behaviour of trustworthy people as it unfolds, than to force them to follow the formal organisation chart. Keeping the relationship architecture simple and the business units, or groups small, also allows for individuals to make a visible personal difference.

---

[a] Sherman, Stratford. "Wanted: Company Change Agents". *Fortune*, December11, 1995, p10

THE FOURTH SHIFT: Feedback creates a SMART organisation

Trust is essential for feedback to occur. Feedback is essential for accuracy of response, learning, and speed of response. Accuracy and speed are essential for Change Efficiency.

Self-Motivating Articulate Resourceful Teams (SMARTs) need face-to-face meetings at every level to generate the quality feedback needed to integrate and change systems fast. Robust healthy feedback is liberating for everyone. It's like discovering that you have a sensitive neural network deep within the firm's architecture, which exists to capture new knowledge, share it, understand it, then act on it. Feedback systems like this, in biology, raise each organism's ability to choose. Feedback across a species, raises the collective intelligence to successfully adapt.

The feedback-action chain should become an almost spontaneous routine, before any risky pro-active changes are attempted. Get these basics right, early. Welcome a few new ritual habits around a new culture. Then agree and go for some 'stretch' goals.

In *Why to go for Stretch Targets* Shawn Tully[a] compared cases at Boeing, Mead, 3M, and CSX. We have interpreted his advice on how to stretch. First, you set a clear, convincing Long Term corporate goal; e.g. earning the full cost of capital. Secondly, you translate this Long Term corporate goal into one or two specific stretch targets for managers, such as doubling inventory turns. At the same time, you all benchmark outside, to prove that the tough goal is not impossible, and to help associates get into the fighting spirit. Finally, you get out of the way!

Chairman Emeritus Frank Shrontz of Boeing believed that they could radically reduce the time needed to build 747 and 767

---

[a] *Fortune,* November 14, 1994, p83-90

planes. Building these Boeing's took 18 months in 1992. Shrontz asked for a target of 8 months by 1996. Speeding up production, reduces inventory. That cuts costs. To convince his people Shrontz benchmarked GE which turned inventories in its heavy manufacturing operations at least 7 times a year, while Boeing turned its $8 billion inventory only 2 times a year. This reality embarrassed Boeing managers. Shrontz incited them to form teams and study the world's best producers of everything from computers to ships. The teams found solutions to reach the stretch goal. By 1994 Boeing could build 747s & 767s in just 10 months!

Drill the teams to handle unfamiliar, unexpected challenges, just like a fire brigade. The point is just to start, and then deal with reality as it happens. Define a goal and invite some specific people to commit to reach it. Start with the rough basics. Democratise from the top, and after some healthy conflict, participation can grow upwards from the roots of the organisation. Let the old structure evanesce and fade, as people begin to perfect the new organisation, by using it themselves.

For example, Microsoft wrote most of Windows NT using only the rough Windows NT code. It was a massive job to create and then integrate the millions of lines of code, and required 250 programmers working alone or in small groups. They called the centralising anchor of their organizing process 'Eating your own dog food'. Essentially, they submitted new code each week to 'The Build Lab' and then took away this new code, to write more fresh code. They used their own product to perfect the product.

Management today is a permanent experiment. You will learn most about organisation from similar experimental changes in your own organisation. Scale the risk, pick good people and just do it. Learn as you go.

An organisation is as sick as its secrets

Secrecy, especially about sensitive information, is typical for many business organisations. When organisations consider downsizing or relocating, the people are often the last to know. Witholding information can result in heavy costs (departure of excellent people, strikes, negative publicity, expensive 'golden handshakes' and destruction of trust, which is essential for the future of the organisation). As Shawn Tully of Fortune Magazine writes, 'honesty is the best management practice'. Dilbert's Scott Adams would probably add, 'but it's the least practiced!'

Some executives in the aggressively competitive IT industry take a trust approach. When 3Com considered to outsource a specific work function, they immediately informed the people in that function. Managers told them that they would decide within 9 months' time. They invited their people's feedback and promised them monthly updates. 3Com also announced that if they were to outsource, the current function-holders would have 2 weeks to decide whether to take a severance package of 2 to 3 months pay, or to take a temporary position until they found a new one inside the company. Some employees left 3Com in advance of the 9 month evaluation. Still, they informed the company on time and regularly updated 3Com about their activities. In 3Com's case, trust breeds trust.

People transform organisations, but organisations change only when people change. The first people to involve in a transformation are the managers. The managers have to learn how to leave the traditional comfort zone of control, punishment and rewards. Depending on your existing culture, a critical mass of key managers must be supported and rewarded to learn how to accept and to welcome difference and diversity, not sameness and conformity. As previously stated for large-scale change you need a critical mass of about 1/3 of your middle managers to become change leaders.

For many established managers, difference and diversity, over loyalty and conformity, is highly counter-intuitive. Headhunters also agree that many companies are not interested in diversity in recruitment, but would rather take on a 'younger clone of the main operating team.' Yet, when change is required, diversity is crucial!

Start with the people who are already for the changes. Go for some credible results with them. This trains them to train the others in this new way of working.

Fear of conflict and negative feedback is the traditional executive nightmare. Oxford Alan Fox once said that 'conflict is endemic', which means it won't just go away. Healthy conflict often signals real concern, also it shares information power, raises the trust level and sometimes puts people into enduring relationships. Conflict is a sign of vitality. The idea of healthy open conflict may not be well-received in certain cultures (especially Asia) where outward expressions of harmony and face-saving are historically essential.

Don't shoot the wounded

Five steps are normally required to transform dependent employees into inter-dependent associates, and managers can expect upline conflict at step three. Get it out of the system and into the open.

The steps are:

1. Dependent. Waiting for orders (baby).
2. Semi-Autonomous. Mobile and curious (child).
3. Counter-Dependent. Attacks authority figures (adolescent).
4. Independent. Experiments with relationships (young adult).
5. Inter-Dependent. Joins groups to handle complexity (mature adult).

Welcome negative feedback

'Companies that hope to reap the rewards of a committed empowered workforce have to learn to stop kidding themselves...for companies to change, employees must take an active role not only in describing the faults of others, but also in drawing out the truth about their own behaviour and motivation.' [a]

Prof. Chris Argyris

See conflict as a challenging risk, not a painful chore, because it builds essential trust. Open criticism is a delicate subject in traditional business cultures, and a taboo in some national cultures. But the evidence is overwhelming, that if real emotional energy is blocked or not channelled effectively, people just won't feel able to take the risk to really commit themselves fully. In a modern world class organisation, no healthy criticism means that something is seriously wrong with the communication channels and probably, the culture.

Secrecy and cynicism are the typical outcomes of some recent change programs. *Move-Up*, Europe's careers guide, ran an article on an influential carmaker, entitled 'Perfect Harmony between Man and Machine'. In the article two engineers and a production manager expressed unshakeable confidence in the carmaker's future. The production manager was the proud designer of the company's local TQM system. He said 'in a highly competitive environment, such as the car industry, total quality of production is a MUST. That's why (our company) invested $243 million over 3 years time to build the most advanced modular assembly line.' A year later the company's head-office decided to close down the facility!

The Management of a pharmaceutics merger decided to close 24 of its 57 facilities (42%), as part of a 5-point plan to boost profits.When a local GM was asked if his 1000 employees had to look for another job, he replied that he had no information about

---

[a] *Harvard Business Review* July/August 1994, p85

the 'restructuring'. Such evasive language games of hide and seek, can destroy trust and make successful change impossible.

Reality-test old assumptions

Once the trust level raises in a group, real creative problem solving can begin. Start by checking out the 'sacred' assumptions. Ask dumb 'what if...?' and 'why?' questions, like consultants and children do. It should be fun with no holds barred. Laughter and play go hand in hand with creativeness. Humans are naturally creative, watch any bunch of kids. You don't need to stimulate creativeness, you just take the blocks and obstacles away. Seriousness and formality at the wrong time is death. Find simple fun ways to remove blocks and break the ice. Companies often use trained creative facilitators or they train executives especially for this job.

What are you really selling? When a large manufacturer of lighters was losing market-share, executives had a fresh new look at the customers and the competition. They realized that many customers purchased their lighters during the Christmas season to offer as gifts. People were actually buying gifts, not lighters. Once they realised that their product was not just competing with other lighter firms such as Zippo, but with similar price range gift articles such as Parker Pens, they were able to reposition their marketing strategy more effectively.

This book was typed on a modern high speed computer equipped with a QWERTY keboard. The QWERTY keyboard layout was actually invented by Christopher Scholes in 1873 to slow the typist down! In those days the machines used to jam if people typed fast. We don't think the same problems exist today on high speed Pentiums!

Obsolete assumptions are mostly a question of habit, attitude, misperception, or bad information. Start to invite and welcome criticism as a challenge to improve operations and culture. Create a regular open forum. Authorise everyone to voice or transmit internal complaints, or those of customers, with no blame or guilt. It's the issues that are important, not the persons.

Pierre Wack, a former senior planner at Royal Dutch/Shell describes how the role of Group Planning as 'provider of information', changed to that of 'questioner of assumptions' in the 70s. In the days before OPEC, Shell managers saw a rosy future for the oil-market. For them, it was 'more of the same' even if the facts provided by Wack's team painted a different reality. Wack's team asked managers to tell them which assumptions had to be fulfilled for their rosy future to come true. Shell managers still assumed a steady supply of oil, steady demand and strategic control by the oil companies. It became clear to at least one third of the managers that the future would be different. It would be characterised, among other things, by a decrease in oil supply and a sellers market dominated by countries united in OPEC. Fortunately, Shell adjusted its business strategy (e.g. it accelerated its development of oil fields outside OPEC) and came out of the oil crisis ahead of several of its competitors. We invite you to (re)read Peter Senge's *The Vth Discipline* (Chapter 10: Mental Models) for a thorough analysis of hidden assumptions[a].

Our in-company 'Change Masters Programme' invites people at all levels to surface and reflect upon their own pet assumptions about customers and competitors in detail. We have even flown batches of trainees over their customer's and competitor's property in helicopters, to help them to collectively formulate a more realistic direction for their own organisation. The future can never be determined. Still, we can prepare for possible scenarios now. It is not important to be good at predicting the future, which is impossible. It is important to deal with the future by understanding and sharing the feeble signals of change in the reality of the present. Thorough rehearsals of 'what should we do,

---

[a] Or read about Shell's 'Scenario Planning' in Pierre Wack's articles in *Harvard Business Review*: "Scenarios: Uncharted Waters Ahead", September/October 1985, p72; and "Scenarios: Shooting the Rapids", November/December 1985, p139

if this starts to happen' type scenarios, help our clients to develop their own collective signposts for adaptive flexibility, which contribute greatly to their overall 'change efficiency'.

Most associates and customers will feel guilty about openly complaining. Support them to overcome this embarrassment. They must gradually understand that this information is vital to the integrity and the culture of the whole organisation. Trust is essential to creativity. People must be free to talk about the negatives as well as the positives. Creative suggestions by everyone in the organisation allowed German chemical giant Hoechst to save $15 million in a year. About half of the 26,000 ideas were put into practice and rewards to people totalled $189,000. Vedasto Arboleda, HR Manager for 3M in the Philippines, offers two other success-stories. One was a secretary's idea for a baby bottle cleaner. This product was test-marketed and became an immediate world-wide success. The other was of a Marketing Manager who came up with the idea of a 3M booth permanently located in a big mall. Before that 3M didn't have a good way to showcase its products. Now the booth approach has been adopted by 3M globally.

Reward honest mistakes

Working in a great organisation is an upbeat feeling for everyone. It's a demanding, often paradoxical mixture, of disciplined seriousness and great fun. You're going to have to experiment if you want change. That means that things will go wrong sometimes. How you handle and learn from failure reveals the true spirit of the winners. No 'turkey' means taking no risks. Like they do at 3M, reward the 'turkey' of the month, gladly! The NASA culture rewards people who admit mistakes fast. The count-down procedure before the launch of the Space Shuttle, allows anyone at any level who thinks there's a failure somewhere to cancel the launch. With the right cultural and executive support, this is a most effective way to avoid future disasters.

Seek pardon before permission

'An established sense of fairness serves as an organisational safety net for risk takers.' [a]

C.A.Bartlett & S. Goshal

Moving from low trust, contractual values towards high trust means accepting risks and initiative and forgiving honest mistakes. Preach the old Jesuit principle that it is better to ask for forgiveness than to ask for permission.

Often rituals and rules have developed in order to absorb[b] the uncertainty of business. Cross-cultural sociologist Geert Hofstede writes that these rules...

'...do not make the future more predictable, but they relieve some of the stress of uncertainty by creating a pseudo-certainty within which organisation members can continue functioning.'

Memos and reports often 'contain no information that anyone will act upon'[c], they are just a ritual device to artificially stop time' for a moment. Sometimes accounting systems, may provide so much detailed information (attempting to reduce uncertainty) that it becomes impossible to find the strategic essentials. Accounting information like this is often used to give an after-the-fact rational justification for decisions that were in fact not taken rationally.

Learn names and make friends

Change the rituals. Executives should take their ties off and go at least three levels down regularly. A Canon executive sent a clear

---

[a] C. A. Bartlett & S. Goshal, "Changing The Role of Top Managers", *Harvard Business Review*, Jan/Feb 1995, p93

[b] Verluyten, S. Paul. *A Course in Intercultural Communication in Business and Organisations.* Acco, 1996, p198

[c] Hofstede, Geert. *Culture's Consequences. International Differences in work-related values.* Beverly Hills-London, Sage, 1980, p159

message throughout his organisation when he started calling customers personally. Learn names and make friends. Work with people, eat with them and listen, to learn from them. Open up the information system. Simplify the language and symbols of your measures. Educate business literacy. Take the lid off.

Jack Stack, author of *The Great Game of Business*, and on the Inc. list of 25 most fascinating entrepreneurs, dramatically turned around ailing Springfield Remanufacturing Corp. (SRC), an American engine remanufacturer. Stack wanted his employees to understand money. In the early 90s, 'SRC spent $300,000 on financial training, this was six times what they spent on upgrading production skills.'[a] As Stack put it:

> 'I needed to teach anyone who moved a broom or operated a grinder everything the bank lender knew. That way they could really understand how every nickel saved could make a difference.'

His open-book management paid off: SRC earned 6% pre-tax on sales of $100 million, and this in an industry with 'millimeter-size' margins. Today SRC is a far different business from the one we studied in the early 90s. In fact, it isn't one business anymore, but rather more than a dozen separate businesses operating under the umbrella of SRC Holdings Corp. The company as a whole does about $178 million in sales, and that 10 cent share of stock is worth $87.36. Yet some things haven't changed. People still play the Great Game of Business, which has continued to evolve. And while 10 of the 13 founders have cashed out, Stack remains.[b]

Executives at Motorola have calculated that each dollar invested in employee education yields a $33 return. Motorola invites employees to invest at least 5% of their time on education. In 'The Age of Unreason', Charles Handy argues that this should be 20% for managers. And there is a lot of education needed.

---

[a] Fierman, Jaclyn. "Winning Ideas from Maverick Managers". *Fortune*, February 6, 1995, p42
[b] *Inc.*, April, 2004, 25th anniversary issue.

According to the McKinsey journal (No4, 57) 97% of the American population is scientifically illiterate, and Americans are supposed to be ahead in the use of new technology!

Understand and have the courage to unlock the repressed 'boss' fear and hatred of past generations, or it will kill your firm today. Build an in-touch culture of face to face contact and emotional honesty and watch a miracle happen around you. Direct open feedback transforms cold remote power and control, into personal influence and trust. Judge leaders by the respect of their followers. Don't tolerate executives who don't respect their own people, or who don't have their people's respect. This is what worker empowerment also means.

Organize with Ciao: the goodbye tradition

Many an old respectable assumption or past success formula will have to be buried with grace and dignity as a matter of routine. Set up a blameless and supportive funeral system and a horizontal fast track. Speed and quality comes from having a big dustbin. Let your people recycle what they think still has some usefulness. During 'The Great File Crunch', Ricardo Semler and his people had a thorough look at Semco's filing system. Anything which was not of immediate or practical importance, or, could be acquired through someone else was thrown out. This policy freed up a lot of space (about 70%), and time and skills (e.g. secretaries whose job consisted of 'stamping pink sheets and placing them in blue folders' were retrained in more productive skills.)

A horizontal fast track makes sure that good people in wrong functions don't just rot away, or eventually leave the company. If a financial expert wants to get involved with marketing, give her that chance. At Semco a minimum of 2 years and a maximum of 5 in a function are standard. Afterwards people usually rotate. This also includes the major shareholder Ricardo Semler.

Changing the wheels of a moving car, while running it at full speed

Essentially, the kind of organisation that you will need to do this is a 'Chaotic Dynamic System with a Self Organizing Feedback Loop', and that's what we're going to build and run, in the following chapters.

2

Two Strategies of Change

'In terms of commerce....intuition will replace rationalisation as the primary source of data in the development of long term strategies, the means of implementing those strategies, and the resolution of everyday challenges.' [a]

Gary Zukav

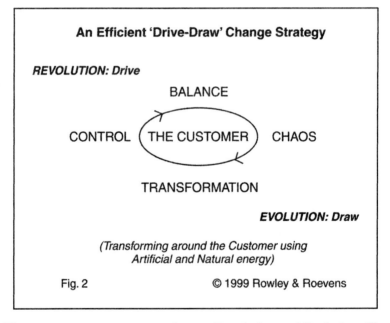

An Efficient 'Drive-Draw' Change Strategy

REVOLUTION: Drive

BALANCE

CONTROL (THE CUSTOMER) CHAOS

TRANSFORMATION

EVOLUTION: Draw

(Transforming around the Customer using Artificial and Natural energy)

Fig. 2   © 1999 Rowley & Roevens

There are two ways to create change; Revolution and Evolution. The model below uses Revolution and vision to drive change, and also

---

[a] M.Ray & A.Ringler, *The New Paradigm in Business*, New York: Putman, 1993, p241

Evolution and values to induce, or attract change simultaneously. Customer focus provides the strategic reference anchor.

Revolution strives towards known goals

Revolution is a man-made change strategy which normally only succeeds in a temporary transfer of power. It is based upon assumptions of control, domination and superiority, which drive powerfully and rationally towards a pre-defined vision. Essentially revolution is a conventional warfare model that seeks to win'. It follows an old map.

Evolution avoids limits and obstacles

'.....nature does not evolve towards goals but away from constraints.' [a]
Stewart Brand

Evolution turns the path into the goal. Natural elements like silence, time, spirit, space and emotions attract, induce and govern its movements. Essentially it responds naturally to change. The simple core operating values seek only to create freedom and choice, and to go round obstacles. Here's an example of this principle as an applied strategy, used by a Grand Master chess player, *'...he found that each move they acted 'robustly' by trying to keep their degrees of freedom as open as possible while still taking possible steps to win.'* [b]

This compass model of car driving, and Grand Master chess, does not focus on scoring a tactical win, it seeks only to stay in the game and to continue the challenge. A win naturally comes with merging and exhausting the finite energy of opposition.

---

[a] Remark attributed to Stewart Brand by Kees van der Heijden ex-Shell Strategic Planning Manager, *Fortune* 16/10/95, p93
[b] E. M.Leifer, *Actors and Observers: A Theory of Skill in Social Relationships*, Garland, NY, 1991

Once leaders can confidently back off , the transformation is underway

'Today, facing competitive pressures an earlier generation could hardly have imagined, managers need employees who think constantly and creatively about the needs of the organisation. They need employees with as much intrinsic motivation and as deep a sense of organisational stewardship as any company executive.' [a]

Chris Argyris

If the Amazon basin is turned into a desert, Nature will be indifferent to it. To Nature, a desert is just as natural as a rain forest. Evolution is indifferent to tactical goals. Stretching this metaphor; Strategic Leaders must learn when to develop a similar paradoxical indifference to performance problems and operational decision making at the Transformation breakpoint (The Attractor phase), if true empowerment is to occur. Just leave the increasing complexity to committed self-organizing teams.

Low Trust limits operational size and damages change momentum

Trust must replace supervisory, or systems control as people gradually learn to self-organize more of their own work. Psychical and material ownership of both the pleasure and the pain attracts high quality personal commitment, which can be directly linked to customer satisfaction and also challenged against competitor benchmarks. Low trust leadership prevents the natural Transformation of the Evolutionary phase. Chaos can also come from a rapid growth strategy in some firms. Low trust also defines and limits any organisation's true growth potential and thus its effective long term operational size. Let's now put some of this into a more practical context.

---

[a] *Harvard Business Review*, July/August 1994, p84

Part 3

REWARD LIKE SHAREHOLDERS.
MANAGE LIKE CUSTOMERS.

Who can change your organisation: Managers? Consultants? Experts? No, only your customers and your own people can effectively change the organisation. Customers and working people define what your organisation is, what it does (or should be doing), and how well it does it. In this section we explore the importance of customers and the necessary mental shift from an employee to an entrepreneur attitude. When your people know exactly what your customers really want and when they are truly enthusiastic about providing it for them, you have a solid marriage around which continuous Change can happen quite naturally.

1

Customer-Driven Change

MIT's Tom Malone '.....contrasts two ways of co-ordinating human activities: markets and hierarchies......computers encourage the substitution of markets for hierarchies....by reducing the cost of comparative shopping....'[a]

'Why are we in business?' This is the typical question every business-person asks. What is the purpose of a business? Well, the purpose of a business as all executives are aware, is to increase shareholder value. Making the shareholders successful is an essential outcome, but it is not an organisational goal. The next question then is, what is the purpose of a business organisation'? This calls for a different answer. The purpose of a business organisation is to make its customers successful. This is in fact a very worthy and practical organisational goal. These two questions describe the dilemma that many business leaders face. Executives must focus on each next quarter earnings, or else the shareholders become nervous, and also keep a watch on long-term earnings, from the customers of today and those of the future, or else the business itself may not survive. Senior executives are often caught in a bind by these two issues.

---

[a] "The Incredible Shrinking Company", *The Economist,* 16/12/90, pp59-60

Today's chaos mostly comes from the customer.

What particular brand of customer does your organisation prefer ? You've got to learn to choose your customers carefully in the information age, because customers have become fussy. The customer of today knows a lot more about what's available from your competitors than the customer of the past ever did. They're well informed and spoiled by other industry standards, so they naturally expect your organisation to deliver the finest value for money, on the planet. This simple fact, has precipitated a lot of chaos into the global marketplace recently.

It's also wrecking firms that are too slow to wake up and respond to the challenge of changing and running their business in fundamentally different ways, at a completely new pace.

Change is blind without a customer focus

A business organisation exists primarily to make its customers successful. To compete today, many firms are learning to tailor their organisation from the inside out, to fit each customer like a glove. There are three types of customer in any firm. Some are real and some, only imagined:

- The Customer of the Past. They got you to here, but they won't get you to there. This ghost really needs creative solutions.
- The Customer of Today.They just want you to be easy and superbly efficient.
- The Customer of the Future.They don't know who they are or what they want until you show them.

In order to understand more clearly what your customers are buying from you, we suggest that you apply a practical perspective inspired by Fred Wiersema and Michael Treacy, authors of 'The Discipline of Market Leaders'. Wiersema & Treacy present the concept of 'Value Discipline', which differs from a traditional strategic approach, because it looks at a business from the customer's perspective of its product and service value. Once your people can identify these values, they can work backwards to shape individual and team decision making.

There are only three basic value disciplines, and your firm must absolutely excell in one of them, although customers will expect you to be up to standard in the other two. The three value disciplines are:

- **Operational Excellence** (efficiency)
  Aimed at acceptable quality, low price, or easy to buy. Usually by direct selling. Focus on optimum supply chains, or high speed production routines. Centrally planned, standardised, tightly controlled organisation. This culture hates waste. Examples: Dell Computers, Aldi supermarkets, McDonalds.

- **Product Leadership** (innovation)
  Aimed to make their own products / services obsolete, first. Focus on invention and fast to market commercialisation. Loose experimental risk taking organisation. This culture seeks opportunity and creativity. It doesn't punish failure, or target blame. Examples: Microsoft, 3M, Design Hotels, Disco's, Mobile phone operators.

- **Customer Intimacy** (tailor made solutions)
  Aimed to win lasting customer loyalty. Often creates its product or service on the customer's own premises. Delegates decision making to people who are closest to the customer. Develops deep client education, understanding and relationships. Open sharing collegiate culture of information and experience. Examples: Top level Management Consulting, Hospitals, Law firms, 5-Star Hotels.

What your customers want to buy from you is often a complex mixture of affordable, easy to get, novelty, or specific solutions to their unique problems. Most of your customers will choose to do business with you for one dominant characteristic, one value discipline, which they feel that your firm does best. This main preference by your customers must be well understood by your staff. Once people really know 'why' certain things matter more than others, they can then naturally develop and maintain the best organisational set-up, to deliver it consistently.

At convenience stores like K-Mart in the US, or Aldi and Colruyt in Europe, customers receive good value at the best price. There are no jingle-bells or baroque ornaments in the products. Goods and services are presented as 'Cheap and Cheerful'. People working in these companies commit to deliver a dependable routine.

Novelty seeking customers want the latest things. Often they don't care about price so much as the innovative aspects of the product or service. In an innovative firm like 3M, 40% of their revenue comes from new products that are less than four years old. Customers interested in experiencing the latest aspects of something, buy from 3M. The major 3M goal is to make its own products obsolete before its competitors do. This requires flexible, creative behaviour in an organisation committed to innovation.

Nike customers don't buy sports shoes, they buy Nike's. A pair of Nike's is presented as the most technically advanced delight for your feet. Innovators often also have to invent the market for their new products. Another example of novelty is 'Red Bull', a fashionable and comparatively expensive soft-drink, which claims to boost the consumer's late night-club stamina. Does it work? Some say it does, but most young people probably drink it because it's relatively new.

The third value discipline does not look at what the market wants, it focuses on delivering specific expert solutions to a customer's unique problems. These customers want a firm to give them more depth, more time and more of a feeling that they are the only customer. Most clients for this discipline would not choose to depend on the cheapest, or most fashionable, medical or business help or advice. These solution providers will go the extra mile for their clients. Confidence and deep relationship building definitely comes before cost here. Typical solution-oriented organisations are specialist software writers, non formula consultancies, and high quality medical services.

Wiersema & Treacy argue that in order to become, or to remain, a Market Leader it is necessary to be the outstanding provider of one discipline and good in the other two. The main point however is to get everyone in your firm involved in discovering how they personally contribute to deliver your specific type of customer value. The organisation can then be facilitated to self-organize and be safely allowed to change and grow outwards, with cash customer value as its central seed.

> '...value discipline is a central act that shapes every subsequent plan and decision a company makes...,from its competencies to its culture...value discipline...defines what a company does and therefore what it is.'[a]
>
> M. Treacy & F. Wiersema

It is important for everyone in your firm to know what your customers are buying from you; what do they value that makes your firm different? Then to help your people to focus on delivering that value superbly well, at a profit. These days, people in your firm should individually aim to become the champions of their industry and to make your value proposition outrageously attractive to customers. The insights of current Chairman of Corporate Governance in the Netherlands, former Unilever CEO Morris Tabaksblat, indicates just how powerful such customer attractors have become. Already in 1997 he told the International Association of Advertisers (IAA) that:

> 'producers no longer dictate customer choices. The era of push-marketing is definitively over. It is time for pull-marketing.'

---

[a] "How Market Leaders Keep Their Edge", *Fortune*, 6/2/95, p52

Unilever's staff have set up several experiments to attract and communicate directly with their customers and to get to know them better. One is an inter-active TV-commercial campaign for Dove soap. The other is a website called 'Mama's Cucina' which promotes Ragu spaghetti. Surfers can read Mama's favorite recipes. They can also learn about Italy, study Italian, and talk to other pasta and Italy fanatics. Unilever's people have created their 'virtual community' to attract, entertain and inform, and also to learn from customers.

During a presentation at Management Center Europe, Philip Kotler, recounted the story of an American lady who wished to buy a Ford car for $17,000. Her local car-dealer would not go below $20,000. So this lady did what every sensible American does, she logged on to the Internet and placed a message which read:

> 'Who wants to buy a Ford for $17,000?' Within 24 hours, 25 people had replied. This lady then printed out the information, went off to her car-dealer and negotiated a group-discount of $3,000 per car!'

Continuous efficient change is competitive

Clear customer focus combined with change efficiency are the two keys to unlock your firm's competitiveness and promote its long-term survival. Change is easy, but change efficiency needs a few fundamentally new ideas about organisation. We have developed the concept of change efficiency to indicate that change is a continuous process and that it is important for modern organisation to embody the seamless ability to adapt and change, along with its market. People often talk about change as if it was a one time event, but a business organisation today has to learn to become continuously changeable, simply to keep existing customers. Your firm must become sensitive enough to be able to respond to customer shifts, faster than your competitors, and keep on doing it. The first one to get into shape reaches the critical mass lock-in first, and can thus win on lifetime customer loyalty.

'...cement lifelong relationships with customers...Rather than relying on dealers to handle all customer contacts, Ford has put up a Web site...The company then routes the customer feedback from the Web site to its marketers and designers to help them plan new products. In the design process, the Web brings 4,500 Ford engineers from labs worldwide together in cyberspace to collaborate on new projects. Next, Ford is going to roll out a system for ordering parts from suppliers...the company hopes to transform the way it produces cars – building them to order rather than to forecast.' [a]

S. Hamm & M. Stepanek

It's often cheaper to stop doing the wrong things

When you can identify precisely what your customers care about, you create an internal change compass.This fixed point of customer reference can guide both what to do and what not to do in your organisation. It's simple in theory. In practice it's messy because it must be physically embedded into your culture. Everyone has to get involved with customers to realise and feel what is important, and what is not important about their jobs, and to the total business. What you decide to stop doing is often more important than what you do, especially when things get a bit chaotic. It's like deciding not to hit the brakes or the gas when the car goes into a skid. You just look and try to point where you want to go, and well,... you trust.

---

[a] S. Hamm & M. Stepanek, "From Reengineering To E-Engineering", *Business Week*, 22/3/99, EB11

$$2$$

Managing a Flock of Cats

'There was a strong element of the merchant in me. I was continuously preoccupied with business schemes. I would look into empty shops, speculating as to what profitable businesses I could make of them, ranging from fish & chips to grocery shops. It had always to do with food. All I needed was capital – but how does one get capital?'

How does one get capital? Many entrepreneurs ask themselves that question.This quote did not come from McDonald's Ray Kroc, or Chocolate Chip Cookies' Deborah Fields nor from any other famous food entrepreneur. Charlie Chaplin wrote it in his autobiography. Charles, born 16 April 1889, was a typical entrepreneur. At age 10 he was already thinking about innovative ways to earn money. He had to. His brother Sydney and he were raised by their mother, a cheerful, loving actress who, due to malnutrition, often went through periods of mental illness. Hunger was normal for the boys. So was survival. After a tough childhood, Charlie worked as a travelling comedian and an actor for several years. He left Britain for the USA. There he realised that motion-pictures were the future, and California the place where it all happened. Most of us know the rest of his story. We suggest you read *Charles Chaplin, My Autobiography* for a detailed account. Charlie was a multi-talented dollar-millionaire. He directed his own films, acted in them and later on even produced them. He wrote the music to his films and founded United Artists.

In the previous chapter we described how customers are changing the concept of a business organisation. In this chapter we explore the difference in roles and relationships between people when everyone is encouraged to start to think and act like a customer focused entrepreneur. As their former employees develop into entrepreneurs, managers will have to develop new coaching roles, too. It will be down to them to spot the talent and to make champions of those entrepreneurial people, who will form into teams to tackle a complex project, and then dissolve these teams to regroup for further projects. A critical mass of mobile project entrepreneurs, will be the most successful asset that any modern business organisation can have, especially when it must deal with continuous change in a chaotic global environment. It is important to understand just what executives will be dealing with, as they simultaneously liberate, and also keep, this kind of energy focused.

In this chapter we present the concept of 'under-management'. We will also describe the history of the entrepreneur, and explore how to promote the actual shift from employee behavior to that of the entrepreneur.

Entrepreneurs require under-management

'....what we are building is a web of trust and shared understandings.' [a]
John Sealy Brown, Xerox Research Centre, Palo Alto

Organisation transformation starts with the people, then it spreads out into the systems. Commit 100% to the people you've already got in your organisation and they will commit to you. As a Manager, you should put together teams of people who trust you, not the other way round. Make sure that people feel secure enough to talk back to their superiors, in all honesty. Eventually, as their new reality dawns, those people will self-organize and run the type

---

[a] *Business Week* 8/2/93, p39

of organisation that they need, for themselves. Remember, we are describing how to fundamentally convert a conventional hierarchical business firm into something much more urgent, robust and better suited for today's global business conditions.

Create an evanescent virtual hierarchy

To shape the build of a new change culture within the existing organisational framework, volatile market forces must reach into, and 'touch', every person in the organisation. 'What you do' can then start to become 'Who you are'. Boss-focused employees must get face to face exposure to some flesh and blood customers, if they are to learn to become customer-empathic entrepreneurs. Feeling the customer's level of satisfaction, rather than the boss's, provides a strategic point of common reference. Understanding your firm's major customer value discipline, anchors the Balance between efficient Control and experimental Chaos, and will also facilitate the iterative Transformation from creative adaptive Chaos, into new levels of high performance commitment and Control.

Begin with volunteers. Include people who really want to prove themselves, to themselves. This is a stretch goal scenario, which no one, by definition, knows how to do. The rewards for success should be very attractive, but to encourage persistence and risk taking, no penalties should attach themselves to failure. Some things cannot be taught, they can only be learned, by experience. Your people will have to learn how to self-organize for themselves, by being encouraged to experience it first-hand. There is no place for over protecting paternalism in a sink or swim business environment. People have to strive to find their own way, in their own way. If they feel technically inadequate for the job, they can request special training and coaching support, but that initiative has to come from them. It cannot be spoon-fed in the usual way that training is provided. Likewise, obtaining additional resources should also test their initiative and ability to improvise.

The prime objective is to get people to accept responsibility for themselves and the quality of their own work, and to pay them well for first class results.

Once people can accept the responsibility for their own training and development, they are learning to 'become that person who can get the things that you want'. This statement represents the entrepreneurial shift towards empowerment and individual transformation. To cope with rapid change, and to maintain size without mass, many organisations have literally set people up in business for themselves, and then become their major client. Educating entrepreneurship creates a network organisation of suppliers.

Every business once started with an order. This order was from a customer, not from a boss. Before an organisation's culture can shift 180 degrees to face outward towards customers, many of the old inward looking practices and habits must be directly changed. Top level understanding, plus visibly demonstrated support is thus essential before you can realistically expect confidence and buy-in from the people below[a]. Top leaders may say what they want done, but they should not say how they want it done, beyond defining some limits, like for example, within the law. This means a profound shift in the historical assumptions, attitudes, language and values which underpin traditional employee management and the supporting human services. Let's take a look at some of these basic changes.

'Why do I always get a whole person when all I want is a pair of hands?'
Henry Ford

To 'employ' originally meant to 'use' someone in exchange for wages. According to the Oxford dictionary, there are four ways to 'use' an object, or a human being:

---

[a] We have produced a one hour audio cassette on the psychology of the entrepreneur, it's called "The Wisdom of Success"

- Handle as an instrument
- Consume as material
- Exercise into operation
- Freely avail oneself of

This is where the offensive term 'Human Resources' comes from. Just like 'downsizing', it strips people of their humanity and turns them into objects to be manipulated, or even eliminated altogether.

A History Lesson: Big windows and clock time thinking

'Using' people became popular with the time based system of work. Look at any old 18th Century factory and you'll notice that it's got big windows. The original owner of the factory was limited by the hours of daylight to maximise production and repay the banks. His hired workers were mostly country people who were accustomed to a different way of working. When a job like the harvest needed doing, they would work unstinting long hours, but in the Winter they would often take things easier. Country workers think nothing of chatting for a couple of hours. They are task, and not time centred. This cultural difference between 'event' time and 'clock' time caused a lot of trouble and misunderstanding during the mechanising of working people. Nowadays, we've inherited the same problem, but in reverse. Today industry needs complete human beings and distributed intelligence once again. The old factory time clocks are coming down with the walls. The mechanical slave days are over in the winning firms.

Merchants understand people... Mechanics understand systems

Think of a business organisation as a mix between the Merchants and the Mechanics. The Merchants deal with new business and unexpected circumstances as they arise. The Mechanics on the other hand must deal efficiently with running existing stable or mature business.

Giant organisations of human Mechanics only grew up over the last century or so, to handle the complexity of big deals. Before then, a Merchant only had a few (2-10) clerks in his counting house, but he also had a large global network of trusted agents in every major port.

Agents bought and sold for Merchants locally, adding value, in a whole chain of deals. For example, cotton from Atlanta might be shipped to England to be woven into cloth to be sold in Alaska for Whale candles to be sold back in Atlanta. The Merchant's profit was in the difference between the buying price of cotton, and the selling price of candles.

Globally, we're moving back to a Merchant network system of organisation based on trust, except everything happens faster. The modern PC has decimated the ranks of human Mechanics and transformed their role. In some industries lightning fast electronic deal chains make it impossible even to buy from some suppliers without first having a fully integrated systems capability. It's a new club, and you just don't get access unless you're accredited. Today, the computer is the Mechanic of the Merchant.

Merchants at the far ends of the world have been able to benefit from their locations, and the new Mechanics', from their new technology. Moldova, an ex-Soviet Republic, Guyana, a South-American region , and also the Netherlands Antilles, plus several other peripheral locations are doing well. Their revenues from telephone sex chat-lines, on-line gambling, and unregulated financial transactions are up. What's caused this success? Well, because of the short-dialing codes of these services, punters think they are dialling a domestic long-distance number, rather than an expensive international call!

Turning employees back into natural entrepreneurs

Many executives still think that they can motivate other people, and they consequently feel responsible for satisfying the needs of their employees. Because of this root psychological paradigm, executives actually recruit and train people who accept and fit that image, and really think of them accordingly, as dependent children. Acceptance, over many generations, has produced a self-fulfilling prophecy of mutual dependence. Most executives genuinely feel protective of their people, and their employees feel a dependent gratitude, often mixed with a deep suspicion. They then behave accordingly, either as needy and helpless, or hostile and resentful of the power inequality. The latter is the more psychologically healthy of the two responses, given such a situation. This is because both parties are not aware of any other option.

Try to see someone's personal motivation as an outcome of how they view their own situation, not as something which can be caused or manipulated by someone else. In other words, shift the responsibility for a person's behaviour back to the person themselves, not other people. It's not what happens to you that matters, it's how you interpret what happens to you that makes all the difference.

We once heard a story about a pilot who was shot down in Vietnam and was captured by the Vietcong. This unusual man made an internal decision to use, what others would call a serious misfortune, as a personal learning experience. After many years of captivity he was eventually released and reported that it was the greatest experience of his whole life; far better than any University education. This man gave his situation a why, and a purpose. He behaved in a pro-active way and used what would probably have killed many other people, to explore his own hidden depths of strength, courage and endurance. The outcome was that he lived through it, and emerged as a healthy and much wiser person.

106

Pro-active people see opportunity everywhere. They naturally accept and welcome all reality and move towards it. Change invites diversity. There are no mistakes in the universe, only opportunities to bifurcate into new directions. We label things as 'mistakes' because they are not part of the original plan. To avoid terminal disaster these days, we must expect 'mistakes', adjust to accomodate them, and learn fast. We must look to our potential, not to our history. Once this is understood, a high performance organisation can re-train ordinary people to start to think and act pro-actively, like entrepreneurs.

What motivates entrepreneurs?

La Rue T. Hosmer, defines entrepreneurs as, 'People who like to get challenging things done in new and unchartered ways despite factual uncertainties and external difficulties, using their individual capabilities.'[a]

As complete human beings, we all have our own dreams and hopes, so these traits can actually be discovered within most people. For historical reasons, working people just don't usually think of their job, as a way to realise them. In a modern organisation which enables, rather than constrains people however, such limiting assumptions can be coached and changed. Below we offer you a list of some typical Entrepreneurial traits.

- Take A Risk.
- Accept And Celebrate That You Are Different.
- Create and Follow Your Own Vision.
- Intuitively Do Things In Your Own Image, Style & Way.
- Exercise Personal Control, Ownership and Free Choice.
- Allow Enthusiasm and High Energy To Flow.

---

[a] La Rue T. Hosmer, "Entrepreneurship – A Guide", Michigan Business School, 1991, p5

- Do Things Well To Complete Your Own Destiny.
- Honour Relationships Based On A Love Of The Business.
- Be Ruthless In Service.
- Create Identity, Self Respect, and a Reputation.
- Make a Visible Difference.
- Expect Financial Independence and Share Happiness.

If you look at yourself, you will probably recognize some of these traits. Senior Executives may also recognise more of this entrepreneurial profile as matching their own, as they rose in the old hierarchy of their firm. These same values must be cascaded and nurtured downline. We will suggest how in section 4. For now, take a look at some further expressions of both the spirit and the substance of entrepreneurship:

In 1996 computer distributor Ingram Micro offered to pay its new CEO, Jerre Stead, $1.5 million as base salary. He refused. Instead he wanted stock options for 3.6 million shares. Ingram Micro went public in October 1996 at $18 per share. A year later this had gone up to $28.5. After a further climb, the January 13, 1999 share price had dropped to $33.5. When Stead retired from Ingram Micro in 2000 it had grown from an eight billion dollar company to a 30 billion dollar company doing business in over 120 countries.

Smart business owners give stock options to their entrepreneurial staff. If not, they would probably leave the business and start on their own. Bill Gates makes many of his people dollar millionaires. According to a 1992 Wall Street analysis, 2,200 of Microsoft's 11,000 employees each held at least $ 1 million in stock. It took about five years of hard work to become a millionaire in Microsoft.[a] As Charles Handy has pointed out, 'Knowledge workers truly do own the means of production

---

[a] Justin Fox, "Free Money", *Fortune*, 7/7/97, p29

today. Your major asset is inside their heads, and they're free to walk out of the door... Karl Marx's dream has finally come true, but not in the way that he expected'.

Richard Kovacevich Chairman and CEO Wells Fargo & Company (which merged with Norwest Corporation) granted options for each employee to buy 100 shares of Norwest stock at $38. He said:

'The impact on people is far greater than I expected...They think there's more value in the options than there really is: It's free and it's just sexy. You get these things only the fat cats got.'[a]

In 1978 Toys 'R' Us gave 15% of its shares to executives and store managers. By 1982 the share price had increased in value twenty fold. Then CEO Michael Goldstein said:

'Options are great, so why not give them to everybody?...This will be a great motivational tool.'[b]

Reward them like shareholders. Manage them like customers

The message for the future is: reward them like shareholders, and manage them like customers. Although Entrepreneurship is common in the USA where individual achievement is valued, it is not an exclusively American phenomenon. At Siemens Nixdorf Information Systems in Malaysia for example, recruits are immersed in a three-day induction program that introduces them to the corporate culture and fires them up with entrepreneurial work attitudes. HR Manager Ahmad Abdul Ghani says that 'we bring in customers to give their views of the company'. This drives home the point that the customer ultimately pays the recruits' salaries.

---

[a] ibid, p29. Stanford Business School Alumni Association, 2006.
[b] ibid, p30

> *'Everybody wants to succeed...I always tell employees that they should not worry too much about what their superior tells them. I say, "Go ahead without waiting for instructions...Go ahead and do what you think is right. If you make a mistake, you will learn from it. Just don't make the same mistake twice." '*
>
> Akio Morita, founder, Sony Corp.

We hope you are beginning to recognize that in the new global knowledge and service economy, the market will weed out individual and organisational imperfections. This means that to survive and thrive in it, almost everyone will eventually have to think like an entrepreneur. Perhaps also even in bureaucracies.

At the start of each new class, we tell all of our own business students this:

> 'My friends can call me professor', but I prefer that you call me by my first name. Start to think and behave like a business person, from now! I am not your parent or teacher today, I am actually your customer. Deliver great work to me and I will stake my own reputation on you, and reward you with the grade. Don't waste my time writing safe bureaucratic stuff, I have to read it all (twice), and I'm a busy person. Get real. Give me real intellectual food to help me in my own research. Tell me about the business world as you really see it. And tell it immaculately well. If you still feel that you are only here to please mum or dad and to get a piece of paper, fine, just keep out of the way of those people here, who do understand what I'm telling you. I will grade you partly on how well you teach me, and also your own colleagues here will do the same. We are all here to learn together. It is a matter of survival for us all...'

If you are a lecturer, a coach, or a teacher, try this new role reversal for yourself, and experience what an amazing difference it can make to the level of commitment, creativity, fun and actual performance.

On graduation, we advise our best people to consider joining businesses that foster the entrepreneurial mindset. Strategist Michael Porter advises people to join the market-leaders. These are not necessarily the household names, they are 'companies that are ruthless specialists, tailoring all their activities to serve narrow market segments in ways that cannot be easily imitated by

110

competitors'. When we think about Germany, most of us know the big names: the chemicals giants such as Bayer, BASF and Hoechst. We certainly know the large car-manufacturing groups, from Mercedes and BMW to Volkswagen. But do you know sunroof manufacturer, Webasto, gelatine producer, GDF, or, cigarette machine manufacturer, Haumi ? Probably not. Nevertheless these three companies have one thing in common: they are all world market leaders. According to Hermann Simon, author of *Hidden Champions*[a], it is Germany's 'Mittelstand', the small and medium-sized businesses, that are the drivers of the German economy.

The big-name companies like BMW, Bayer, Hoechst, are reducing their workforce, but new jobs are being created in the factories and workshops of many small and medium-sized enterprises. Entrepreneurs really provide the life blood for the German economy.

In this section we have examined how customers and entrepreneurs are fundamental, to both understand and deal with change in your business. What you are actually attempting to liberate, attract and transform is:

- The fruits of ripe chaos, in terms of new: people, projects and high performance.
- Turn Workers into Suppliers.
- Time work into Event work.
- Individual commitment to customer value.

Essentially, customer centered change will attract the entrepreneurs, not the politics. In the following section we will indicate the nature of some new kinds of executive tools that are available, to successfully nurture and transform an organisation. Basically, these are organisational tools which resonate and amplify, rather than tools which cut.

---

[a] *Harvard Business Press*,1996

'Controlled disequilibrium is a better strategy for survival than coherence and order.' [a]

Prof.John Humble

[5000 people were together at a chaos conference, all controlling the movement of one single plane simultaneously, in a large digital flight simulation] '...Then the entire group of 5,000 co-pilots, as if inspired by a single thought, sends its plane through a graceful 360-degree roll that would make a top gun proud. The room erupts into a standing ovation...Nobody was in charge...The conferees did what birds do: they flocked.' [b]

Kevin Kelly

---

[a] reported in *Forum 90*, AMA 13/6/90, p7

[b] William C. Taylor, "Control in an Age of Chaos", *Harvard Business Review*, Nov/Dec 1994, p65

Part 4

PRO'T'US: THE CHAOS CONTROL LENS

This section consists of four parts. Part one examines the dynamic architecture of organisational change and explores two key phases: 'Efficient Control' and 'Creative Chaos', to understand how they 'Balance', and also may spontaneously 'Transform'.

Part two develops more depth on the role of rewards in motivation. Part three takes the four dimensions of a change which were presented in the Introduction', and explores each dimension: Enhance, Perturb, Attract and Excite, in a more complete organisational context. To end the section, part four adds the shifts that occur in Leadership approaches. We then present the complete strategic change lens as a full model, which we call 'PRO'T'US'.

1

Introducing Pro'T'us

Forget the clockwork universe

'Disorder can play a critical role in giving birth to new, higher forms of order. As we leave behind machine models and look more deeply into the dynamics of living systems, we begin to glimpse an entirely new way of understanding fluctuations, disorder and change.' [a]

Margaret J. Wheatley

Almost all Fortune 100 firms implemented some kind of change-programme over the last 15 years, investing on average $1 billion per company. Only 30% of these efforts actually improved the bottom line, compared to the cost of capital. Also 50% failed to improve their market share.[b] Something is wrong in the present change business to deliver such poor returns on such a substantial level of investment. There are four reasons why any business organisation would deliberately seek to change itself. They are:

- To catch up – these firms are being driven by an often urgent external pressure.
- To lead and maintain its lead – this is a deliberate form of strategic positioning.
- To rejuvenate itself – this often means regaining the agility to adapt to external changes.

---

[a] *Leadership and the New Sciences*, San Francisco: Berret Koehler, 1992, p11
[b] Niton Nohria – Harvard Business Service paper No. 96-054

115

- Routine updates – no problem here, these changes are internally generated and usually involve no more than a technical or maintenance overhaul.

The first three reasons for change, all focus on what is happening in the external environment. As you can now appreciate from what we've discussed so far, the increasingly chaotic nature of the modern business environment means that these kinds of changes call for something which is different to what most companies are used to. Business as usual is over, in three out of the four cases above.

'Business is about creating change for other businesses.' [a]

Andrew Grove

Let's re-cap on some key issues that were mentioned earlier. First, it is now evident that when the environment begins unexpectedly to shift and change chaotically, you have to use a quite different conceptual model of organisation to be able to understand and to deal with this new situation effectively. The mechanical command-control hierarchy was actually designed and built to resist and to fight change, not to welcome it. It doesn't work well embedded in the chaos of the new information age. In practice it's too slow to recognise and adapt to the significant discontinuities which characterise the new business reality, because it rests on the wrong assumptions about the nature of reality itself.

For the last hundred years, scientific management has assumed that chaos just leads to a mess and that a firm disciplined, mechanical hand was required to bring it under control. The word 'management' itself comes from the Latin 'manus' meaning hands (so does 'manacle'), but you need more than just people's hands, to survive today. Many of these antique scientific ideas, though

---

[a] Grove, *Only The Paranoid Survive*, Doubleday, 1998, p20

116

brilliant in their day, are actually over three hundred years old. They date back to Sir Isaac Newton's 'Mathematical Principles of Natural Philosophy' (1687). Mechanical control models work well for regular systems like simple inter-planetary trajectories, simple engines, and firms focusing on Operational Excellence. They don't apply to the kinds of discontinuities and shifts which characterise the far from equilibrium conditions of business today.

Hierarchy was an organisational machine. It was like a great castle built on sand. It gave the comforting illusion of permanence, equilibrium and great strength and it was thought to be impregnable, until the cannon first appeared in the 15th century. Overnight, the sands of history shifted and the castle suddenly became obsolete. Undermined, and rendered deeply unstable by new technology, it fell into ruins. Today, the computer is something like the cannon, except that its target can move. To hit a moving target you need a smart self-directing missile, not an old fashioned ballistic cannon ball. Organisationally speaking, that's where people's ability to self-organize comes in. People are not in the organisation today, the organisation is inside the people. They are the organisation.

Change invites diversity not sameness. Trying to predict and to control information-power in an open complex changing environment, quickly leads to loss of control. Monolithic central command and control forms of organisation give way, in the information age, to distributed intelligence. This simply means that a person is not closely directed by The Organisation. Rather she and he are only given broad outline guidance and then liberated to find their own way. Organisation thus evolves within the person, according to whatever must be done. When everyone understands both the big picture and the purpose, they can take advantage of fresh opportunities in the field, and can fully exploit the broken plays, which will inevitably arise.

Let chaos reign, then rein in chaos.[a]

*'...the old order won't give way to the new without a phase of
experimentation and chaos in between'* [b]

Andrew Grove

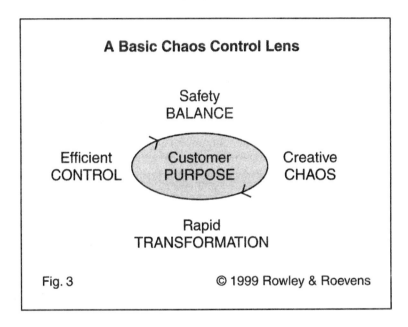

A Basic Chaos Control Lens

Safety
BALANCE

Efficient   Customer   Creative
CONTROL   PURPOSE   CHAOS

Rapid
TRANSFORMATION

Fig. 3   © 1999 Rowley & Roevens

Look to the left on the above chart. 'Efficient Control' indicates a phase where an organisation operates efficiently, smoothly and fairly predictably. People do what they must do to produce a consistent outcome of profitable results. This is today's cash cow, but it may also become tomorrow's arena for change. Looking now to the right, 'Creative Chaos' indicates the phase when your

---

[a] "A High Tech CEO Updates his Views on Managing and Careers", *Fortune*. Sept 18,1995, p141
[b] in *Only the Paranoid Survive*, p130

people are exploring and trying out new ideas. Hopefully, some enthusiastic people have been busy experimenting with alternatives, long before the old ways no longer work. Some inefficiency and slack here is essential to creativeness. It gives the thinking time to try, to test, and to perfect.

Generally, as far as change goes, the people who make money are more important than the people who count it. Change should therefore be focused more on what a firm makes, rather than on how they measure it. Measures and records, may not be permitted to change much, so a protecting firewall must isolate them from perturbation. Permanent efficient control is necessary in some specific functions in any organisation. Obviously the business basics of accounting, tax, or the legal records sections cannot run chaotically, for example. These public activities must conform to fixed external standards, so they are not ideal candidates for much internal change.

You don't cut the dedicated Head Office people either, just like everyone else, you educate and involve them in the whole strategic picture. Just because control is being devolved, does not imply that many of these former controllers cannot be allowed to find useful work for themselves in the new organisation. Fear is not a good way to engender the spirit of creativity, open communication and personal internal commitment that you will need for a deep fundamental transformation. Anxiety and fear will lead, at best, to only cosmetic change; doing more of the same with less. It creates a stressed out empty shell of a firm that everybody hates, including you and eventually, probably, your customers and shareholders, too. A house at war with itself cannot stand. Education and re-training is a more robust long term strategy for organisational survival.

'Chance, or what might seem to be chance, is the means through which life is realised. The problem is not to blame or explain but to handle the life that arises...The best advice is to take it all as if it had been your intention – with that, you evoke the participation of your will.' [a]

Joseph Campbell

Once you learn how to change, it will never stop. Efficient control in production or services, although a necessary part of the business-cycle to generate and to accumulate profit, is always a temporary condition. When many firms all follow the same strategies, these cycles get shorter and the competition heats up. Knowing when to change is like surfing on the ocean, you've got to be able to spot when to jump off before the wave breaks, and to catch the next wave early. Many firms do scratch a living by trying to follow the trend, but it's only a few real market leaders who actually create the wave in the first place. They are known in their industries as 'The Competition'. Market leaders equate serious competition with impending obsolescence, not with challenge. To them, it's just a signal to leave the wave. They prosper on constant creative innovation, not on execution, and they grow fat on short innovative delivery runs, just before they change the whole landscape. Strategically they remember the future, so they are always positioned on the right side of time.

Microsoft is one of the best examples at doing this kind of change, so let's look at how they recently positioned themselves for the internet. Bill Gates said:

'To get a big company moving fast especially on a many headed opportunity like the internet, you have to have hundreds of people participating and coming up with ideas. But you've also got to get them focused, or you'll never get any decisions made or get anything done. Our digital nervous system (internal E-mail) informed and propelled our decision making...on April 6, 1994, I e-mailed my staff to say: 'We're going to make a big bet on the internet.'... We held our first important progress review in August 1994. Once again, it was the

[a] Joseph Campbell, *The Power of Myth*, Anchor Doubleday, 1991, p203

newer employees running the show...One person at that meeting felt that the technical challenges of conversion would be too difficult. The next speaker turned out to have already developed a converter on his own initiative. His manager had told him the internet would never be part of their group's business...By...December 1995, it was damn the torpedoes, full speed ahead.'[a]

This is a good example of a CEO telling his organisation what needs to be done, but not being expected to know, how to do it. What vision cannot compel, only involvement, informed people and self-organisation can accomplish. The rebel in the ranks gets the chance to call the shots. We've looked a lot at the organisational methods and the internal cultures in these IT firms, because they are the models for most industries in the future. They all operate in a hostile fast changing environment. They really know how to manage and to focus entrepreneurial people and they know how to share and to use information, on a large scale.

We compare an IT firm to a tribe. The Chief in the hierarchy of a tribe sets direction and dispenses law, but it's the diverse hunting groups that bring home the food. Leadership in a hunting group moves around according to the demands of the situation. The wise old shaman says where to go to look for the game. The warriors protect the band on the journey. The top shot sets up the kill, and the strong man carrying it back, calls the breaks. When they do get back, the chief then says who gets what, according to their tradition. Effective organisation here is a healthy balance of both teamwork and hierarchy. Today's chaotic business environment demands putting self-organizing resourceful teamwork, before command.

Diversity and difference is a natural resource to a team. Creative individual response to change comes before centalised control. Know-how power people inter-act freely with position power people, like one big team. The chief expects to hear many conflicting opinions when deciding on direction, but once they go

---

[a] "The Day Microsoft Got The Internet", *Financial Times*, 19/3/99, p18

for it, the whole team decides who does what best, according to the changing needs of the situation. Operational leadership then ceases to be one fixed person and becomes a fluid self-organized outcome of the behaviour of the followers. The leader' then just happens to be that person or group, who people rate and are naturally following at the moment.

Change efficiency demands a dynamic fluid organisation, that naturally fits people, not the other way around. In the history of the follower, the human ability to self-organize is far greater than our ability to be organized by someone else. Self-organisation is in fact a much more ergonomic way of working together under conditions of change. It's also people friendly.

Seeing the nature of change from a chaos attractor perspective reveals a range of possible behavioural outcomes. Here are some typical human consequences, to different types and levels of change pressure:

- Repetition locks behaviour to a fixed point. More of the same is a limited cycle attractor.
- Variation involves small changes around a 'torus' bulge, or swelling attractor.
- Adaption describes experiments within the attractor boundaries, around a few bifurcation points. This depends on the robustness or freedom to deal with new external events.
- Transition indicates that a qualitatively different response begins to emerge to crisis and deep chaos. This is an unborn state between past and future.
- Transformation is characterised by the emergence of a more complex and qualitatively different level or way. This is not acting differently, but actually becoming and being a different identity.

The control phase is about repetition and the commitment to efficiently produce quantity. The other four behaviours devolve to the creative phase, which is often characterised by worry, stress, tension and frustration, but it can also involve playfulness, high commitment and individual satisfaction. Most businesses, like everything in life, need periods of Creative Chaos in order to remain healthy. McKinsey's Frank Ostroff asks 'Where do we want to be horizontal and where do we want to be vertical?The trick is getting the balance right'[a] The new question for self-organizing systems today is 'Who should do the balancing?'. Popular Change Management Models, e.g. TQM, BPR, only focus on Balancing 'Efficient Control' and 'Creative Chaos'. They rightly assume that too much 'Efficient Control' stifles innovation. They also rightly assume that too much 'Creative Chaos' hampers efficiency. So most consultants still suggest a mechanical Balancing type of oscillation. With an acceptance and a better understanding of the dynamics of chaos, however, you can now see change as a cycle, which also passes through a fundamental Transformation. It returns to order and control as something quite different, and at a much higher level of performance, than it started out. This is what we've been missing up to now in our efforts to manage change. People must be coached to go all the way through the phase of 'Creative Chaos', before they can Transform the ripe fruit of it, into 'Efficient Control'. This change process is a continuous spiral.

As a manager, you must take a risk and go right through a phase of 'Creative Chaos' with your people, rather than to prematurely stop and to collapse the chaos process half-way, and then try to manage the situation back into control. The problem of handling change, was rooted in the old science assumptions of management, which imagined that chaos was always bad, and must be avoided at all costs.

---

[a] *Fortune* 3/4/95, p64

Every firm is a combination of two distinct organisations rolled into one

One aspect must deal efficiently with existing routine business, and the other with attracting new business, or dealing with unexpected circumstances quickly, as they arise. These days, in many industries, the latter ability is becoming more important than the former. Firms which originally built their business on the economies of scale and long run cost efficiency, are today having to change their organisation and culture to also embrace continuous innovation, and to get full commitment to world class performance levels. A main priority is to get these two systems in harmony and working seamlessly together.

Efficient control maintains your existing mature business as a profitable routine. Chaotic freedom on the other hand, is necessary to create innovative new products and the new markets which attract new business. Also, it's the best way to respond flexibly and fast, when the unexpected happens. For safety's sake, a realistic strategic balance can still be made between efficient control and creative chaos. Too much chaos tears an organisation apart, but too much control and it will atrophy and die. Although chaos itself cannot be controlled, it can be limited. Deciding how much change your firm can afford means that final overall strategic direction and budgetary control will always remain a top executive job.

Strategically you should aim to cut the costs of your existing business, but outspend your competitors to create new business. Be clear about the practical distinction between Management and Leadership in your firm. Management is about 'doing things right'; it deals with the powerful reality of the present like cash flow and efficiency. Leadership is about 'doing the right things', it invests your organisations untried strength in an unknown future, to increase long term stock value.

The way to Creative Chaos, is not like the way back to Efficient Control

Driving targeted parts of a system out of control is a different process from nursing it through chaos, and then drawing it into some form of effective new order. Rudy Rucker, a chaos writer, suggests two good metaphorical examples to show the difference. The journey away from control towards chaos is like the first break shot at the balls in a snooker triangle. On a frictionless table, small differences on the first shot will create big differences the longer the balls continue to bounce around. So at the start, small things matter most. That's one reason why we wrote this book. It's important to be as right as possible first time, on the first break.

Emotions communicate. Coming into order from chaos is a totally different proposition however, it works something like this: imagine a enthusiastic concert audience applauding the end of a great show. The clapping is thunderous but random at first, then a few people start to shout 'More! More!'. Gradually the applause starts to develop the unity of a spontaneous rhythm pattern which demands an encore. 'More! More! More!...' The whole crowd is roaring in time, like one huge creature. That spontaneous, self organizing rhythm outlines the shape of something that a modern social scientist could call an emotional 'strange attractor'.

Rhythm, is a good example of human energy flow, around an attractor. It is naturally hardwired into all human beings, and can easily emerge in the collective spontaneous behaviour of crowds. An emotional attractor pattern like this just appears all by itself. It's a natural phenomena that can't be engineered successfully. Any kind of attractor is a response, not a magnet. A truly great and moving artistic performance only provides the possibility for its appearance. It can't be guaranteed in advance, but when it does happen, it comes together for a while with tremendous impact, only to eventually drift apart, break up and fade.

A busy restaurant on your high street, a popular song, or a fashion, can precipitate the same kind of effect. Timing is so important when dealing with this kind of natural energy. The business trick is to catch it on the rise and leave it before the peak. Knowing what to do is less important than sensing when to do it, or even better, when not to do it. Sometimes it is more effective to keep out of a naturally evolving process, especially if you're the boss.

Managing energy like this is not a new idea to a trained facilitator of group dynamics. It's just never been an understandable transferable skill before chaos theory and quantum physics changed the way that we can now think, as social scientists. Key actions must be appropriate to the change phase, or they may unwittingly inhibit or collapse the natural processes.

Transforming chaos into efficient control

Your organisation's ability to rapidly transform Creative Chaos into Efficient Control is crucial to refine its existing processes and to get new products into new markets quickly. Mostly, this is a natural evolutionary process which must be well understood, before it can be helped. There is no quick fix, just like any birth, it's messy. A culture which allows the free flow of information and opinions however, is crucial. A traditional business culture of non-confrontation presents big obstacles to this free and open flow of information and honest feedback, particularly upline and across departments. To identify your organisation's key information blocks, we suggest this simple system by Thomas A. Stewart[a] for finding your information pools and flows:

- What information drives the (new) business?
- Who has it?
- To whom is it worth most?
- How can it be moved?

---

[a] Thomas A. Stewart, *Fortune* 12/6/95, p76

Doing things like eliminating internal waste is a logical, rational and practical thing to do, but generating and absorbing new business often requires an intuitive leap of faith. Getting these two systems to merge into one; to develop Rapid Organized Cooperation across functions; requires the intervention of a third party of unquestioned authority and common reference, namely the Customer!

'The giving of gifts immediately causes a disparity in status between the donor and the recipient. More often than not the giving of gifts requires a duty to reciprocate.' [a]

Ian Peate

'Today, Ford and its suppliers are building relationships built more on trust than on contracts or ownership positions, relationships that are essential if networks are to function effectively.' [b]

Raymond E. Miles (et. al.)

---

[a] "Gift Trapped", *The Times Higher Educational Supplement* 15/1/95, p7
[b] *California Management Review* Vol 37. No3, Spring 1995, p138

2

The Spirit of Rewards

What behaviour does your organisation reward?

'....whatever gets rewarded will get done.' [a]
Anne B. Fisher

Rewards are a direct way to compliment focused changes into a business culture. Normally they are the first things to examine and change, before you ask people to do something different. For example you must physically create a system that rewards a group of people to cooperate, rather than to compete, before you put them together and expect cooperative behaviour. In this respect, stock options based on total business performance can do wonders in eliminating departmental walls. As we saw earlier, many top US companies use them and the trend is catching on in Europe. Once you can clearly identify what must change, you may wish to specify targets, and then shape up a new type of bonus or incentive proposal, which is coherent to reward the desired behaviour.

Bonuses and salaries are not part of the same package

A bonus is a reward, but a salary is a right. They are not related. A bonus should be as simple and direct as possible. It is a

---

[a] *Fortune* 17/4/95, p78

behavioural tool, not part of the accounting system. It should not be considered as a cost. Salaries are an overhead cost. You can't buy goodwill with salaries, but you can easily create jealousy and competition with them. Salaried pay is not objective. It's people's subjective feelings of 'fairness' that are crucial. Money itself does not motivate for long, but the lack of fair pay can certainly demotivate and offend. Above a minimum amount, the numbers are only part of a symbolic contract.

Already in the seventies Richard deCharms provided evidence that external rewards like money can actually demotivate people from doing what they intrinsically enjoy doing. This goes against the predictions of 'drive theories', which assume that people need continuous new external rewards, e.g. more money, to fulfil a task. Many managers still hold on to those outdated, false drive theories. In *The Hidden Costs of Reward*(1978), Lepper & Greene show us what can go wrong when we start rewarding people for something they already love doing. They may start to dislike the activity! Don't assume that your people want to be rewarded with more money or more responsibility. Ask them all individually, what motivates them specifically.

SAS Institute of Cary, North Carolina, is the largest privately held company in the US software industry. SAS has achieved an employee turnover rate of less than 4% in an industry where the norm is 20%. SAS does not offer more pay. However, they offer intellectually engaging work, a family-friendly environment with exceptional benefits, and the chance to work with top talent using state-of-the-art equipment.[a]

---

[a] Pfeffer, J. "Six Dangerous Myths about Pay". *Harvard Business Review* May-June,1998

Move from contract to trust

'....we see that a part of mankind, wealthy, hardworking and creating large surpluses, exchanges vast amounts in ways and for reasons other than those with which we are familiar from our own societies.' [a]

M. Mauss

The world economy has only two ways to exchange goods or services. Either we give or lend things to people, or we sell or barter them. A gift as a moral exchange, whereas a sale is a contract. A contract shrinks time at the moment of giving and receiving, to an instant. Trust and spirit is squeezed out of a contract exchange. Time itself is in fact contracted'.

Trust is a gift of time

For example, if you meet a friend and you buy them dinner, they will morally 'owe you' and they will probably remember it. They will carry the spirit of your gift until the next time that you both meet. Then, they will probably insist on taking you out, or giving you something, and thus complete their end of the exchange. Many cultures don't even have words in their own languages for buy and sell, because they never thought of it as a way to exchange goods and services. They probably will have words like borrow and lend however. Gift exchanges occur among friends and in families all over the world. When you accept a gift, you also accept the spirit of that gift. This is a moral obligation to repay it somehow, or to pass it on to someone else. This is the basis of the world's black economy. The time when you're supposed to repay a gift is seldom known, or exactly agreed. Morally, that's up to you (or it just happens automatically, for example leaving a legacy, when you die).

---

[a] *The Gift-Forms and Functions of Exchange in Archaic Societies*", London, Cohen & West, 1970, p27

Send your Change teams out bearing gifts

Where salaries can incite jealousy and unfulfilled neglect, pure gift recognition can light wholesome fires of desire among onlookers and well wishers. Generally, you don't pay for new ideas, you just expect them. They're a kind of gift and should be rewarded in the same spirit. With profit sharing and stock options, they will show up in the purse anyway. Give people gift objects as tokens of personal recognition and get the leaders to do the same.

Keep all the deals and standards simple, open and clear. Basically, you can't work fast without honest feedback and high quality mutual trust. Choose your people well, but expect and budget to get ripped off sometimes, too. GE's Jack Welch accepted the Kidder Peabody fraud with a shrug and a '...shame on us for not spotting it sooner.' He still assumes that most people keep their faith. With high trust organisational values, it's inevitable to get burned sometimes, but the benefits of travelling light far outweigh the costs today. In a self-organizing climate and with more direct reports, you can't possibly control people's work closely. Low trust here can actually seriously limit your career. High trust and good judgement is the measure of the great. Be great!

3

Seeding Organisational Change Efficiency

'....pushed to change the way they work, most people push back.' [a]
Anne B. Fisher

'...the evolution of most industries is highlighted by two phases, the fluid and the specific. During the fluid phase, industry leaders focus on product innovation...during the specific phase, which tends to follow a brief transition, process innovation subsumes product innovation. Industry leaders shift their focus to production efficiency, which results, paradoxically in a product which is more useful and easier to use.' [b]
(i.e.refined)
James Utterback, Mastering the Dynamics of Innovation

Now we're going to put what we've discussed so far into a more practical context, and suggest a new way to handle the transformation of chosen sectors of your business. This is a method to understand:

- what you're really getting into,
- where to plan
- what to watch out for
- how to read change as it happens in your organisation.

The four dimensions of change, discussed below, will give you the

---

[a] "Making Change Stick", *Fortune* 17/4/95, p75
[b] J. William Gurley, "Why The Network Computer Stands a Chance", *Fortune*, 12/5/97, p119

key aspects of the new lens. You can then use it to identify and link any proposed actions (or non-actions) of your own, with their likely effect on the total change process itself. Interventions should be coherent and kept simple.

'During one of his two combat tours in Vietnam, Federal Express CEO Frederick Smith got a quick lesson in survival from a crusty marine sergeant. 'Lieutenant,' the sergeant told Smith, 'there's only three things you gotta remember: shoot, move and communicate.' Smith quickly warmed to that advice.' [a]

We want to emphasize again that this is a lens of Probability. As a manager, your job is to coach your downline people to become successful, in their own terms, and to link this to cash customer appreciation. They do the work of change, not you. You can only intervene to improve the chances of coincidence; to reinforce the behaviors and strategic outcomes that you welcome, and also to protect and to avoid collapsing things too early. All this can never be truly predetermined or absolutely certain. With this lens however, you are not simply condemned to watch helplessly, as a chaotic landscape unfurls. As your in-depth understanding of the whole change picture improves, your own behaviour will also become much more change coherent. In our view, given the state of real science, what follows is about as good as it gets, for any manager today.

Planning for a journey is different to actually taking it. Taking a transformational change in real-time, does not conform well to a mechanical model of levers and drivers, because you're not actually driving. Your people are. On this trip, you navigate far more than you steer, so it's ok for you to relax a bit and sit back to watch the road for any big turns, or new developments. Your lead people will get better at driving change the more they practice. An

---

[a]Linda Grant, "Why FedEx is Flying High", *Fortune*, 10/11/97, p 86

experienced driver needs to do very little to keep the car going straight, compared to the wild erratic over-steering efforts of a novice. Like any truly creative journey, fundamental change means that you can't possibly know where you're going when you start out. Some firms never come to accept this, so they never even get started.

Revolution may begin with a specific vision, but the unfolding architecture of its evolution is actually built on a process of spontaneous unpredictable outcomes, most of which are unmanageable. We've already mentioned that one large consulting firm claimed that it can predict any organisation's behavior. We honestly feel that this is misleading and it's also scientifically impossible. Aiming to liberate space, human energy and diversity, by recognising emerging reality and removing the limits to fresh opportunity, is a far more robust change strategy, than these dangerous illusions of certainty. Prepare your organisation to get lucky and to recognise it.

Three chance accidents

1. The vulcanization process for rubber, which made possible the manufacture of automobile tires, was discovered by accident when Charles Goodyear spilled a beaker of laytex and sulfur on a hot stove!

2. The creation of penicillin, which started the use of antibiotics in medicine, came about when Alexander Fleming carelessly contaminated a bacteriological culture with bread mold.

3. A compound that Pfizer was testing for angina was supposed to improve blood flow to the heart. When the medicine was tested on a group of male college students they kept getting erections – result Viagra.

The Four Dimensions of Change

The transformational change process contains a mixture of both manageable and spontaneous outcomes. In evolutionary theory, environmental changes can trigger a reproduction / extinction cycle of resonance and interference, around the existing, or new attractor patterns. When you observe how a natural system changes, by human intervention, or by some accident of nature, four dimensions to the overall system's behaviour, can be recognized. Things will happen in each dimension which cannot be predicted. Yet they are clearly capable of classification, as belonging to a particular change dimension. The flow of events runs as follows:

* Something new or unexpected happens out there which produces major changes in the environment. This will ENHANCE a pressure for the total system to change. The desktop PC for example, changed the nature of the whole computer industry. What Andy Grove of Intel would call a 'Strategic Inflection Point', had arrived.

* The old ways of doing things no longer work effectively and PERTURBations occur which drive the system to initially self-organize itself into chaos. This turbulent process also releases a diversity of new untried types and behaviours out into the world. They contest and collaborate, in a kind of pragmatic experiment to survive.

* Small adaptive advantages and irreversible luck will eventually appear to accrete, to cluster and to repeat, around a particular group or type of mutation, as if ATTRACTed. From a manager's perspective, they can be recognised as weak patterns or 'sensitivities' that spontaneously emerge out of the creative chaos soup. Like fresh new shoots appearing, they may require some protection from the frost in the organisational climate.

- Finally, because low energy systems cannot self-organize effectively, you can intervene to help their growth. Energy and resources can now be imported to EXCITE synergy and to support the lead pathfinders of these embryonic breakthrough projects. This is aimed at gaining critical mass and at refining and perfecting processes, to produce output.

'Is the leader really a leader, or is he simply the one out in front on a wave?...one who perceived what could be achieved and did it.'

Tolstoy, War & Peace.

Remember that what the physicists call 'Attractors' are not magnetic. They are un-causable. Think of them as an outcome of vectors, like for example the way that a village can grow in time, around two paths which happen to intersect in the woods. They definitely cannot be planned for, or predicted. Rapid recognition, protection and maximum organisational learning must be allowed to occur around this critical Attractor dimension, if you are to eventually market the fruit of all that Creative Chaos.

Four facets of the Strategic Change

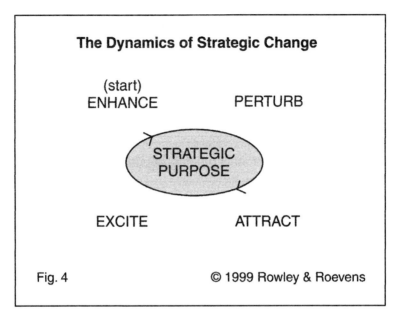

The Dynamics of Strategic Change

(start)
ENHANCE   PERTURB

STRATEGIC PURPOSE

EXCITE   ATTRACT

Fig. 4   © 1999 Rowley & Roevens

The above flow describes an interwoven process of relationships between four clear dimensions, which model and shape the dynamics of a changing system, as a whole. Because we are actually looking at non-linear phenomena of infinite complexity, it is impossible to predict specific outcomes, or even to clearly see where one dimension stops and another begins. But these four dimensions can act as a guide, for what the whole system is likely to do next. These are the four facets of the lens. Any contemplated intervention can now be tested for its coherence, in the full context of all four facets. When applied to a business change programme, it looks like this:

- **ENHANCE** – The change pressure, team/customer rewards & probability of coincidence.

- **PERTURB** – Spontaneously the system enters turbulence & releases its diversity.

- **ATTRACT** – New people, projects and/or performance levels, will begin to emerge.

- **EXCITE** – Synergy and symbiosis to generate profitable output.

In practice, you can intervene to Enhance and Excite the change process in the normal way. However, with Perturb and Attract, you are truly prospecting for creative innovation and can only pre-limit the Perturbation boundary and recognise interesting new Attractors, as and when they appear. They need the time and space to ripen and to grow. These two unpredictable spontaneous dimensions of change will self-organize themselves into, and then out of chaos. They are best nurtured by under-management.

Keep watch, but mostly keep out!

Non intrusive levels of intervention and deliberate non-intervention, are slowly becoming better understood on the leading edge of Western management thinking. The theme of a conference at Aston University (UK) clustered around silence, absence and the subjectivity of relationships. Here is an excerpt from one of the conference documents:

> *'Were it not for the buffer zones and blank no go areas that are created and reproduced on a daily basis, organisations might always be on the cusp of chaos...organisation control, whatever else is involved, depends for its effectiveness upon a distribution of both presences and absences...the idea...is not like that of a switch, sometimes on and sometimes off...I like the way that knitting simultaneously produces a net of spaces alongside its connection...a strong emphasis on absence and silence can be found in contemporary social theory...'* [a]

R. Munro

---

[a] R. Munro, "Connection/Disconnection: Theory and Practice of Organisation Control", *British Journal of Management*, Blackwell, June 1997, Vol 8: S44-61

One CEO who already understands and uses this evolutionary approach in practice is Jean-René Fourtou, who turned around ailing Rhône-Poulenc. He says that:

> 'The creative interaction of unlike minds cannot be managed, only permitted...the most important thing is just to let them meet...sometimes the best management is none whatsoever...Le Vide (the vacuum, gap, emptiness, or void) has a huge function in organisations...If you don't leave Le Vide, you have no unexpected things, no creation. There are two types of management. You can try to design for every thing, or you can leave le vide and say, "I don't know either, what do you think?" [a]

Robert Haas, former CEO and current board chairman of Levi Strauss & Co., says,

> '...I don't have the answers, you don't either. We've got to listen, be open to influence...I believe that if you create an environment that your people identify with, that is responsive to their sense of values, justice, fairness, ethics, compassion and appreciation, they will help you to be successful. There is no guarantee – but I will stake all my chips on this vision.' [b]

Using the four dimensions of the change lens to monitor and to run the details of a change programme, can help you to understand what any particular action is doing in the context of the total change process. Each of the facets can also work together coherently, to 'shape the build' of actions, around a defined strategic purpose (eg. Customer satisfaction, growth, easy to buy, etc.) of a change, and to sequence these actions more naturally.

Classify all proposed actions with qualitative change coherence using these tools. Even a system in deep chaos can be better understood. They also serve to reduce the need for formal control, effort and stress upon senior management which can precipitate and accelerate a more efficient transformation.

---

[a] Thomas A. Stewart, "A Thought In The Shower", *Fortune*, 25/11/96, p87
[b] Stratford Sherman, "Levi's – As Ye Sew, So Shall Ye Reap", *Fortune*, 12/5/97, pp74-77

The 'Steps' of Change

To absorb this approach, we'll take an example, and use the lens. Let's choose a hypothetical situation. Imagine the sequence of practical steps which we could take, to facilitate the transformation of a rigid organisational hierarchy, into some form of flexible, adaptive, high performance, team-based system?

Let's start out with an evolutionary mind-set. We first assume that our hierarchy is already pregnant with the seeds of diversity, creative energy, performance commitment and the natural ability to self-organize itself. We don't have to put these things into the system, they're already there. Like nature does, we use what we've already got, and build on the existing genetic architecture. Our job then, is not to make the system do tricks, it is to understand its true nature, and to stop the things which in the past have prevented these natural tendencies from emerging. Basically, we're aiming to liberate a new type of self-organizing creative organisation, from the chains of its mechanical past.

To accomplish this, we realise that we can only partly intervene sometimes, according to the way that the four dimensions of the change spontaneously develop. We can also monitor the shifting process architecture as it changes phase, from control to chaos and then back once more to a new level of control. Let's explore each dimension, in its respective phase, and suggest some examples of the kind of actions that we could perhaps take.

DIMENSION ONE – ENHANCE

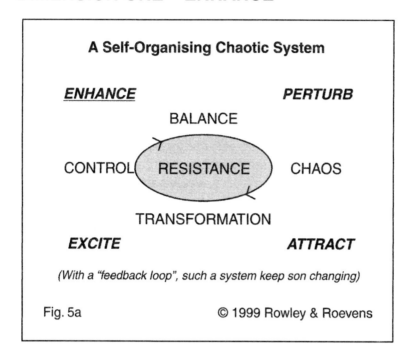

A Self-Organising Chaotic System

ENHANCE   *PERTURB*

BALANCE

CONTROL   RESISTANCE   CHAOS

TRANSFORMATION

EXCITE   *ATTRACT*

(With a "feedback loop", such a system keep son changing)

Fig. 5a   © 1999 Rowley & Roevens

ENHANCE the Change pressure and create a field of change which supports informed risk taking, cooperation and where open self-organizing behaviour can thrive.

The summary below suggests a number of possible actions, or coherent steps, which you could follow to prime an organisation, or unit, for a major change. It is only a rough outline guide to help you to think about, and to flesh out, the details of your own situation for yourself. Clearly, you know the priorities of your own business best. Think also about the other three dimensions (perturb, attract, excite). What could you perhaps do now, to prepare for them?

EXECUTIVE SUMMARY
A List of Possible Steps to ENHANCE the Change

- Secure your own power base and mandate

- Fix Strategic Change Leaders' rewards for team cooperation and overall company performance

- Map and select suitable Change Leaders

- Bring them together as a Strategic Change Team and shape a collective vision.

- They then:
    - Target 3 – 5 specific things to change.
    - Create a Change-Budget. Allocate enough Time, Space and Resources.
    - Change the downline reward system to favour entrepreneurship, horizontal cooperation and customer appreciation.
    - Simplify key measures and encourage the free flow of information.
    - Call regular public meetings.
    - Build a critical upline feedback loop, act fast on good suggestions.
    - Question all assumptions and encourage some experiments.
    - Raise Customer, Supplier, and Competitor awareness
    - Get downline help – Each Strategic Leader seeds an Operational Change Team

AIM: TO ALIGN THE PURPOSE & TO WIN BROAD COMMITMENT

A word of warning first

A profound level of organisational change of this nature, requires absolute personal integrity from all change leaders. You should not attempt this exercise with leaders who are not ready to commit to values of openness, honesty and sharing, and who do not demonstrate a genuine desire to coach other people's success. All company information will also eventually have to become open and available for inspection. The exercise will test and probably change everyone involved, both personally and professionally. Once begun, this kind of change cannot easily be stopped.

In the above outline, the first thing to do is to secure the mandatory power base, to both undertake and protect the full change cycle. Who owns the company? Is it public or private shareholders? Is it a family? What is important for these people: immediate or future earnings, growth, market dominance, etc ? Before you initiate the change, you must either obtain the approval and commitment of the key power-holders, or personally accept the risk, to run it as a scaled experiment and to get the credibility of the results. If you need permission, make sure that the powerful stakeholders understand what a deep Strategic Change really involves. Educate them to feel the same urgent pressure as you, to know why you must change this organisation. Also tell them honestly that change is an investment, which may cost money for a while.

The Enhance dimension, just like the final Excite stage, is manageable. This is where you can prepare as much as possible to go through the other three dimensions coherently. Setting up the 'initial conditions', even if you can't predict specific outcomes, is crucial. Your objective here is to align everyone to the purpose and to win wide commitment.

Once you have a solid go ahead from the powers-that-be, it's time to consider getting help. Work out a new reward system for the first group of primary Strategic Change Leaders, before you even put them together. Fix their rewards on internal cooperation (performance bonus) and total company long-term performance (stock). Then personally select, invite and group these people into a Strategic Change Team. This small group will carry the heart and the spirit of your emerging new organisation. The team should consist of a diverse range of people, holding various levels of hierarchical power and coming from each major functional department. They must be people who trust you enough to strongly disagree with you and to tell you the truth. They must also fully commit to the change, and eventually, to each other. Change Leaders should be focused, determined, willing to break rules, and be well respected by their own troops, or colleagues.

Depending upon the mandate from the shareholders, the Strategic Change Team (with you in it), then debates and sketches out its own collective future vision for the organisation. We emphasize collective. As the boss, you should listen far more than you talk at these meetings. You need to develop the rapport of an initial outline vision together, or else it has no value. As the new vision emerges, you can begin to identify and to share some specific individual tasks of:

- What to do?
- Who will do it?
- When will it be done?
- How to measure and to reward it?

When these activities become clearer, ask each person to specify and to write their own contribution down on one single sheet of paper. Then personally make a deal with them in front of the whole Strategic Change Team, and let everyone have a copy. Once everyone knows exactly who is doing what, you can let them all go off to do it, in their own way.

To help the Strategic Change Team to begin to scale the extent and the risk of the total challenge, each member could list 3 to 5 key things which they want the firm to start doing, and also to stop doing, plus also add what they would personally welcome to happen spontaneously, in the firm. They will clearly understand

144

from the mandate, whether they are aiming to fundamentally transform the architecture of the whole firm, or only to run experiments in the margin. If change is new to your existing culture, sometimes it is wiser to start a full experiment in a subsidiary, or a new aquisition – something like a controlled explosion – and if successful, to transfer the acquired knowledge and skills of the self-organizing culture, back into the mother company. Ford did that with the Ford Taunus project. The Taunus teams became extremely successful in developing new, self-directed ways of working together. Their excellent performance results also gave the early pioneers credibility and status with the rest of the firm. Management then asked them to coach people in other areas of the company.

When the extent of the challenge is understood, the Strategic Change Team then sets an outline change budget to allocate enough time, space and resources. They then create a new downline reward system to favour entrepreneurship and horizontal cooperation, focused on customers. In training and developing this new customer approach for example, everyone could be asked to list 5 things about their own job that cash customers love?

Rumours will spread long before people start to feel the effects of any change. In order to avoid any unwanted 'talent bleeding'; where essential people get nervous and start sending out their resumés; individual leaders can identify and anchor this talent well before the changes start to happen. Give such people enough security and invite them to develop or to find an exciting new role for themselves, or simply discuss how they would like to see their own future develop in the company.

'Without constraints we get utter confusion, but with constraints we get chaos.' [a]

Ralph Stacey

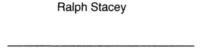

---

[a] op cit., p170

Leaders can also set up regular paid open meetings, to get critical upline feedback aired and out in the open, and also to create a common sense of urgency. To find creative ways to educate people about customers and to benchmark competitors, they must tell people the painful truth about the new business reality; introduce them to real flesh and blood customers and suppliers, and make it personal. With a new downline reward system in place, they can begin to open up the financial information and to start to educate widespread business literacy. Their job is to get as many key people as possible focused on working with the change, not on leaving the company, or on resisting it. A typical problem with secrecy and downsizing is that it destroys real communication and trust and also invites political maneuvering. This creates the wrong kind of self-interested boss fear that destroys change momentum. Boss fear splits people up. People can't work together looking for the opportunity to win in the marketplace, if they feel under constant threat of losing their own individual jobs.

Strategically the team isolates the cash cows. It limits disorder from seeping into areas of the organisation that generate money from existing business, for now. It looks more towards innovations in products and processes to attract new business. Chaos obviously is not allowed into departments that function best as hierarchies.

Educate any hostile change resistance to the new reality of the market place. Use this energy. Encourage people to speak their doubts and fears openly and safely, in public meetings. Open healthy conflict builds trust. This is not about manipulation, it's about survival and reaching world class standards. Assign the most cynical change resistors to go out and to actively benchmark the top competitors, and to visit high performing operations with similar processes to yours. These people need to know and feel the purpose of change the most. Don't fire these people, create the opportunity for them to experience the truth. New Paradigm management assumes that everyone does the best they can with what they've got, and treats them accordingly. Give your people a reputation to live up to. Let them feel proud and honoured to work in your organisation. Enhance the spirit of the change. No deep pessimism among the leaders, beyond this point.

The final suggestion is for each Strategic Change Leader to start to cascade the change initiative down and accross the firm, and assemble an Operational Change Team, comprising of people in her/his own network of known associates, throughout the organisation. Each Operational Change Team will essentially do the same kinds of things that we've suggested to Enhance its own part. This is known as 'training to train'. These kinds of actions will Enhance the start of a coherent change on any scale, from a small department or business unit, to a large multinational corporation, and will naturally roll into the following dimensions of Perturb, Attract and Excite.

DIMENSION TWO – PERTURB

'Phase transitions are turbulent. So in order to change a system from one predictable state to another, nature uses a period of random behaviour in which the symmetry of one form of order is broken and another emerges. Instability is an essential feature of change from one state to another in nature.' [a]

Ralph Stacey

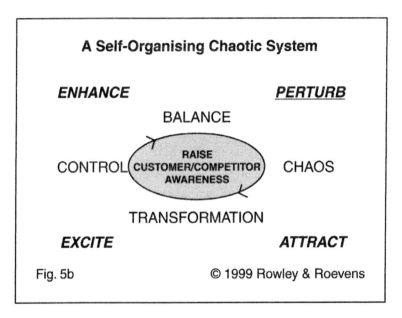

A Self-Organising Chaotic System

ENHANCE   *PERTURB*

BALANCE

CONTROL **RAISE CUSTOMER/COMPETITOR AWARENESS**   CHAOS

TRANSFORMATION

EXCITE   *ATTRACT*

Fig. 5b   © 1999 Rowley & Roevens

PERTURB: 'To facilitate the renewal process, top level managers must take on a new role- one that disturbs the organisational equilibrium. [b]

C.A.Bartlett & S.Goshal

---

[a] *The Chaos Frontier*, op cit., p354
[b] C.A.Bartlett & S.Goshal, "Changing The Role of Top Management", *Harvard Business Review* (Jan/Feb 1995): p.94

EXECUTIVE SUMMARY

Typical forces which PERTURB

Let the Market Enter

- Introduce direct customer feedback on all levels.
- Open, invite and share all strategic market and financial information.
- Communicate and debate any new signals and competitor information.
- Seed diverse new projects and empower people to try.
- Welcome unconventional differences.
- Make a new employment offer based more on results, than time.

Perturb the fear of The Boss: This leads to self-organisation

- Champion open feedback, big meetings, up-line criticism and proposals.
- Abolish oppressive status symbols, rituals, rules and dress codes.
- Encourage people to manage their own time and to organize their own space.
- Invite some teams to elect their own leaders.
- Liberate departmental stockpiles of talent, goods and space.
- Build a horizontal 'fast track'.

Others:

- Seek out fresh opportunity, space, time and resources.
- Train HRM in entrepreneurship and change management.
- Grant paid time for training on demand and individual initiatives.
- Authorise new emerging roles and relationships.
- Protect those who dare, to 'seek pardon before permission'.
- Support down-line operational decision making.
- Employ the intelligent use of executive silence and time.
- Under-Manage – refuse to command and keep out.

AIM TO RELEASE CUSTOMER PURPOSE, URGENCY, COMMITMENT, INFORMATION SHARING, DIVERSITY, SELF-ORGANIZATION, CREATIVITY, RANDOM CHANCE.

'The discovery of new ideas cannot be programmed. This is why revolutions and other social cataclysms often have a positive influence on science. By temporarily interrupting the routine of bureaucratic chores and putting the organizers of scientific research out of commission, they give people the opportunity to think.' [a]

Simply Enhancing the change will produce Perturbations. People will start to think and to behave differently. They will begin to live with more uncertainty, which is a new way of doing things. You don't need to manage Perturbation. It will happen spontaneously as a natural follow-up to some of the actions taken previously. If you want to fuel and accelerate the level of Perturbation, there are certain additional actions that the members of the Strategic Change Team can take, which are included above.

The changing heart of the market has to govern the running of your business, not the fixed pyramid heads. An effective business change should liberate the natural energy that flows from customer love, competitor fear, open information sharing, and self-organized creative experimentation, to get people out of the old comfort zone, to create turbulence, and then to evaporate walls and internal resistance. The dust of change will never settle unless the global competition does. We don't think that it will in the near future. Whatever got your firm this far, almost certainly won't take you deep into the 21st century. You will need a different more dynamic approach to organisation, just to stay in business. Diversity and abundant mutation is how nature deals with change.

Your team could select some unconventional rebels to join them. Who are the odd-balls at your company? The training manager of a famous bank told us that she actively recruits 10% weirdos, people with a Master's degree in pottery, or those who collect live Pythons for fun. Often it is the rebels who come up with new ideas.

------

[a] "Chance and Chaos", David Ruelle, Professor of theoretical Physics, p53

Fully open the company's information. In Semco-Brazil everyone, even a factory worker, knows and understands Semco's financial situation. They follow the firm's results like football strategy. Also, not only do many people tell the firm what to pay them, everyone also knows how much everyone else is making. This may look scary in companies where telling how much you make, is an absolute taboo. It also used to be like that in Semco. But the secrecy did more harm than good. One of the first things Semler did when he took over from his father, was to clear out the filing system. Don't hold on to anything unessential. When you tell the truth, you don't need a big memory.

The opposite is secrecy and departmental thinking. One HR Manager in a big consumer manufacturing firm we visited recently, actually told us that their products weren't as good as the general public really believed they were. He said that their expensive quality brand image was all hype, and that exactly the same unbranded goods, were being made down at the other end of the factory. We didn't even know this guy, for him to say that. If the HRM will tell anybody that, we wondered what the workers might say? That Manager saw himself as 'HR only', not as a marketer for his company. Because of his blinkered departmental attitude, that manufacturer lost two customers. Incidentally he was the firm's Change Manager too – he said it was in his job description!

DIMENSION THREE – ATTRACT

Survey the landscape to identify new motivational possibilities of self-organisation, around which a system will eventually be captured and transformed, into a higher orbit.

'Bifurcation is even more ubiquitous than chaos. Track the bifurcations...'
Ilya Prigogine, in conversation with the authors, 7/1/98

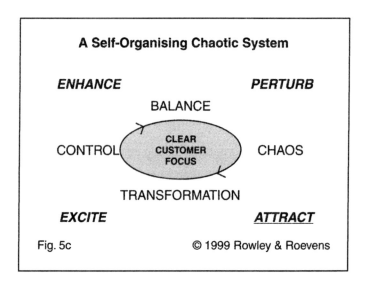

A Self-Organising Chaotic System

ENHANCE   PERTURB
          BALANCE
CONTROL CLEAR CUSTOMER FOCUS CHAOS
       TRANSFORMATION
EXCITE   ATTRACT

Fig. 5c   © 1999 Rowley & Roevens

'Observing the disorder...the mind must be extraordinarily quiet, sensitive, alert, not caught by any habit, physical or psychological.'
Jiddu Krishnamurti

EXECUTIVE SUMMARY

Suggested actions to ATTRACT fresh new outcomes

Possible Executive Activity:
- Recognise promise in emerging projects and proposals.
- Coach individual and team 'stretch' goal setting.
- Educate Business Literacy.
- Commit to make a formal Deal, related to cash customer approval.
- Build relationships that make the Customer successful.
- Authorise committed teams to control their own resources and performance.
- Defend their intuition and the practical use of common sense.
- Recognise the emerging symbols, language and rituals of the new teams.
- Make gift-rewards to recognise the transition from 'clock' to 'event' time.
- Transfer power.
- Promote individuals and small groups to make a visible difference.
- Display a winning indifference to operational process problems.

Possible Team Actions:
- Match customer Attractor values, with the product and the team culture.
- Use the product to make the product. Hold regular 'Build' meetings.
- Fix roles and personal reputations on world class performance.
- Learn from mistakes.
- Let workers become suppliers.

AIM: TO TRANSFORM EMPLOYEES INTO ENTREPRENEURS

> *'The biggest payoff from growth is with people...Without expanding opportunities ...it's impossible to attract the best...I know you can do it, even if you think you can't...find ways to grow!'* [a]
>
> Larry Bossidy, former CEO, Allied Signals (Honeywell)

In the alchemy of change, as a chaotic system spontaneously reaches the Attractor dimension, it can start to generate embryonic new patterns and shapes of discernible order. To see a real new business Attractor, it is important that you are looking for an opportunity, not for a problem. Recognition itself is a psychological process of filtered rejection. It's like seeing a bright yellow flower that absorbs all colours of the spectrum except yellow. The flower itself is not actually yellow, it just rejects and reflects only yellow light. What it actually rejects, is often what reflects to the observer. This what Larry Bossidy sees in the potential of the person, in the above quote. He could see what they often cannot. It stands out from the white noise of all the other colours. When you're looking for growth, it's important that you are continually looking for fresh opportunity rather than problems, because either will act as a filter.

The build is shaped by the election of many outcomes and behaviours that work.

In this Attractor phase, it is your job to watch and to listen carefully, to pick up the faint whispers of promising talent and emerging new projects. Protect what fits, set deals, resource and/or empower, but don't manage. Here are some suggestions of how to do this:

Recognise people's extra efforts with gifts. As we explained in the previous chapter, a gift is not part of the contract, nor is it illegal pay. It is a way to create a new, more profound relationship with your people, one based on trust. Create a gift budget for change leaders but ensure that it's clear that people are rewarded for serving customers, not for pleasing the boss or for competing against each other.

---

[a] Shawn Tully, "...show us how to grow". *Fortune*, 21/8/95, p45-46

Agree how to share added customer value and profits. Fortune Magazine's Thomas Stewart advises investors to check out how widely a company's fruits of success are distributed amongst its own people, through stock options or incentive pay. His rule of thumb is:

'if front-line employees cannot earn bonuses of 10% of salary based on company and individual performance, do not invest.'

Ricardo Semler regularly distributes around 23% of profits to his employees.

Change Leaders agree an outline Deal with individuals and teams, who then personally commit to actually do it. Depending upon the uncertainty of the project and the 'employee' history of the people, there will probably be varying levels of reliability. Trying is the lowest form of commitment, however. Make it clear that any type of deal with you is still a deal. Accepting both the authority and the responsibility for their own word is what really empowers people to give it 100%. It becomes a matter of honour. Where the result of one project must integrate with other projects in your portfolio however, absolute commitment to get the result is required. In such cases, if the people themselves decide that they can't do it, it's still their job to outsource it to people who can. We will talk more about the role of Delivery in the final Excite dimension, but for now you should also be starting to conduct yourself more as an internal business customer, than as a manager.

Let the Teams control their own budget and resources. For example, people should be allowed to arrange their office or work-space according to their own wishes. If they need equipment, they buy it themselves. They don't have to go through the purchasing department and wait for months. They just go to a supplier or a scrap yard and buy or make what they need. This is faster and will often be much cheaper. It's simpler to trust people and to just give them a seed budget, which is also part of the deal. Let them decide how to spend their own money.

As part of the deal, also encourage people to select their own training needs themselves. Educating business literacy for example and coaching employees to think like entrepreneurs, may take some training in basic financial skills. You may recall what we wrote in section 1. When Jack Stack of SRC spent $300,000 on financial training, this was 6 times what he spent on upgrading production skills. Stack's reason was that he 'needed to teach anyone who moved a broom or operated a grinder everything the bank lender knew. That way they could really understand how every nickel saved could make a difference.' His open-book management paid off. SRC earned 6% pretax on sales of $100 million, and this was in an industry accustomed to millimeter-size margins.

Stewart suggests that you invest in Entrepreneurial organisations. In his article 'Cashing in on Trends in Advance'[a] he advises readers to check out how much companies spend on employee education. He suggests you invest in companies that spend at least 2% of payroll on education. The Asian Business Review offers similar advice to investors. A study by the National Center on the Educational Quality of the Workforce, of the University of Pennsylvania, found that each $1 invested in an employee was more than twice as effective in raising the company's productivity as $1 invested in new machinery!

You may involve some active customers during the Attract phase when self-organisation has started to take place around a project. Of course, you don't invite customers to witness a complete mess. Let customers talk to the teams and inspire them.

Make sure that those who feel they need to leave, or, to join a team or a project can do so easily. Although the deals are made individually with the people not just the leaders, teams and roles are not fixed. People can 'buy out' as well as 'buy in'. Let the groups handle hiring and firing themselves. Self-organisation

---

[a] *Herald Tribune*, 1997, p 13

requires maximum flexibility. Real communication can only happen between equals. Essentially, to coach employees to become entrepreneurs, you treat each worker as you would treat a valued supplier. They are like customer equals who have personally committed to an outline Deal.

Some of the new projects may appear threatening to others inside the organisation. It is important for Strategic Change Leaders to protect people and their pet projects, from outside interference. During the Attract phase, you may sometimes directly intervene, in order to support a project's continued growth. Focus on what you are for, not on what you are against. Do not kill the energy of any project which does not appear to fit the overall vision. That vision may itself change. Simply allow any 'duds' to naturally die in the market. Also, such an act may be interpreted as a signal to drive people back into a culture of dependency. If possible, just ignore it, but actively support and protect promising projects. Allow strategy to emerge out of enactment as well as by design. Remain open to influence. Let the cash customers decide.

DIMENSION FOUR – EXCITE...

...synergy and endurance, towards mastery and perfection. Cause emotions which keep vital energy levels up, to continue the turbulence required for a system to find and reach its own higher orbit level.

'Sometimes what a company needs is a group that a manager can't control.' [a]

H.J. Leavitt & J.L. Blumen

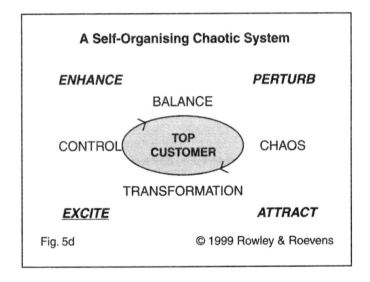

Fig. 5d   © 1999 Rowley & Roevens

---

[a] H.J.Leavitt & J.L.Blumen, "Hot Groups", *Harvard Business Review* Vol./Issue (July/Aug 1995):109

EXECUTIVE SUMMARY

Some interventions to Excite the love of efficient control

Fix and agree a DEADLINE
- Firm up the details of the outline Deal: quality, standards, volume, etc.
- Run the clock backwards to the delivery date.
- Let proud reputations, persistence and acquired skill create efficiency.
- Unexpectedly, gift reward exceptional effort and performance.
- Publicly, light motivational fires of positive recognition under the whole organisation.
- Parade and VIP top teams and individual talent, as the new core identity.
- Fully recognise and resonate to the new culture, language, symbols and rituals.
- Create 'internal' customers.

Collect on all fixed dates to DELIVER.
- Accept only the best, or expect outsourcing.
- Let people freely rise, step down (to study), leave and rejoin the organisation.
- Share the creation of new wealth generously, according to feelings of 'fairness'.
- Celebrate and share success, with trend setting customers.

AIM: THE FIRM ITSELF BECOMES THE TOP CUSTOMER

'...this disconnection of production and marketing into providers and purchasers had its definitive effects on organisation culture...(and)...dramatically changed the everyday life of managers.' [a]

In the fourth dimension you can actively make interventions which will Excite the self-organizing process, and ensure that your people generate enough energy and enthusiasm to turn each developing practice or process, into a new habit. The main objective here then, is to refine and to transform each new project, into profitable enduring performance and output. Each person must psychologically own the challenge, for commitment and creative energy to flow. Effective, purposeful behaviour will naturally follow and your firm will become the top customer of its own working people.

Expect teams to meet their deadlines, and to deliver to standard, or else they must outsource, or you will! Deadlines excite purposeful behaviour, as many students know at exam time. Another way to Excite, is to parade your Top Teams. The Ritz-Carlton Hotel Company describes its business as 'ladies and gentlemen serving ladies and gentlemen'. They treat their own employees like customers. When you enter the staff quarters, the walls don't suddenly turn green or battleship grey, they are spotlessly clean and furnished like the guest rooms. The staff also eat the same quality of food that they serve to guests. Needless to say, people like being treated with respect, and just like in Semler's company mentioned earlier, staff turnover is almost zero and there's a long list of job applicants hoping someday to join the firm. Customers get the best, so everyone wins.

To break departmental thinking and to generate excitement, we mentioned that on one of our own in-company training programs, we put people into teams of 5, and flew them in Agusta Helicopters. The teams included Strategic Change Leaders from all levels of Westerlund Corporation. One team included two top-

---

[a] R. Munro, ibid: S51

managers, a top-management secretary, the head of the dockers union and an ex-director. Another team included a PR assistant, the distribution manager, an accounting secretary, the purchasing manager and an operations supervisor. Although group-leaders emerged during the training, this did not necessarily follow the official hierarchy. Also team leadership rotated depending on the task at hand.

Before they boarded the helicopters, we gave each team a strategic customer-competitor questionnaire. The pilots then flew them over some of their competitors and some of their customers property in the port of Antwerp. This really excited everyone. Of course, many of them – even the tough ones – were secretly scared to enter the helicopter, but they did it anyway. One marketing guy did kneel and kiss the ground, Pope style, when his crew got back and we all had a great laugh. This exercise allowed them to physically and metaphorically distance themselves from their organisation and act as real helicopter view strategists. When we went back to the training room to develop and to make concrete Deals & Deadlines for the chief during the afternoon session, all of the resistance and suspicion which existed at the beginning of the training was out, and people were eager and excited to co-operate.

Another way to Excite, is to celebrate. It coaches people to expect to win. Make each company success a worthwhile and joyful experience for everyone. Light fires under the downline people and it naturally motivates up. You don't motivate people by putting a torch to their heads. When you create heroes, you automatically light fires under the onlookers.

Our training clients receive rough video-copies of the entire training. We suggest that interested members of their teams then compile a company video, to show how the strategy emerged to those people who weren't there. It can also impress customers, suppliers and any new recruits. Touch the product and you feel the organisation. Emotions communicate. You want people to be exited and proud to work for your company.

You Excite people with opportunity and by liberating talent stockpiles. You don't put talented ambitious people in the cupboard, until someone retires and a new management position opens up. Many of them will eventually send their résumés to your competitors. Allow those people to move horizontally. Build a horizontal fast track. If someone is an accounting expert, and they want to have a go at sales – great! – let them be invited by a sales team to go out and do it. If some trusted talent decides to leave your company for a new offer, always keep the return back door open. This is standard in Silicon Valley. Make it a practice at your company.

An effective way to Excite entrepreneurship is to 'sell in the make'. Why don't more companies offer their people incentives to sell the company's products to their friends and relatives and introduce them to the dealer network? Many workers express entrepreneurial skills and organizing ability outside of work, in their hobbies or in the clubs they run. Remove mental and physical walls to allow those talents to self-organize and develop inside your organisation. Much innovation comes from workers and customers, not just from the R&D department.

The Excite dimension occurs, when whatever was targeted to Enhance for change, has successfully transformed and is now moving back towards a phase of 'Efficient Control'. Payoff synergies have clicked and married, and things in that area are drawing into a new, improved level of order. But this is not the end of it. The first successful results will buy you the credibility and punch to spiral, like a healthy virus, deeper and wider into the fabric of the organisation.

Now's the time to plant the seeds for continuous process innovation among the operations people. When organisational change is seen through a chaos literate change lens, and shown to work in practice, people at all levels can begin to understand and fully embrace a new adaptive habit that we call 'Change Efficiency' ™. The powerful emotional experience of really going it alone, as self-organizing individuals, will stay in many people's memories like a battle legend. The experienced converts of the first transformation become prized coaches. They know how it feels to lose the usual and to go after an impossible dream, body and soul; and then to successfully capture and turn that dream into an impossible benchmark, for others. They have acquired a basic new group skill of letting go, to change rapidly and effectively, in perfect tune with the business environment. Each individual naturally exercises internal customer value discipline, without the need for external control. Allow these agents to become the messengers of change to Excite more people to Enhance to Perturb to Attract to Excite, *ad infinitum*...

Pro'T'us

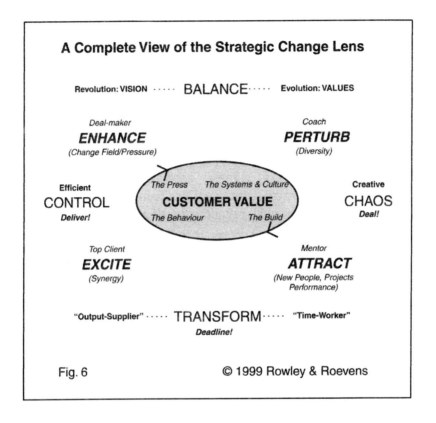

A Complete View of the Strategic Change Lens

Revolution: VISION · · · · · BALANCE · · · · Evolution: VALUES

Deal-maker   *Coach*
ENHANCE   **PERTURB**
(Change Field/Pressure)   *(Diversity)*

Efficient   *The Press*   *The Systems & Culture*   Creative
CONTROL   **CUSTOMER VALUE**   CHAOS
Deliver!   *The Behaviour*   *The Build*   *Deal!*

Top Client   *Mentor*
EXCITE   **ATTRACT**
(Synergy)   *(New People, Projects Performance)*

"Output-Supplier" · · · · · TRANSFORM · · · · "Time-Worker"
Deadline!

Fig. 6   © 1999 Rowley & Roevens

'When you cut into the present, the future leaks out...it tells you what you already knew but didn't know that you knew it.'
William T. Burroughs speaking on BBC World Service radio

The key insight in this book is presented as a holistic lens of the complete strategic change process. It's a continuous spiral that keeps repeating like a fractal pattern, which is similar but never quite the same, each time around. We call it Pro'T'us after the legendary Greek god who spontaneously and freely kept on changing. If seized and held however, Proteus would speak the future. It was the act of letting go which restored to this god of the sea his natural ability, to change and to adapt. An embracing acceptance of today's reality, combined with a decent support system for letting go, unlocks the paradox of change efficiency. Operational values which 'Touch' customer and competitor benchmarks and formally recognise unselfish behaviour, essentially make it a lot easier for people to change.

Pro'T'us exposes the four dimensions of change, along with the major strategic phases and breakpoints, as a complex web of coherent actions and possible outcomes. The first step is to test, to link, and then to lock any proposed intervention, to whatever your particular customers happen to value. With your customers clearly in mind, start to list what you personally want to change in your organisation. Use the Task Centred Change method in the next section of this book. Next, use the environmental pressure in your business to Enhance the co-operation of your chosen group of Strategic Change Leaders, and create the critical feedback loop, to test your own assumptions with them. Go off-site somewhere to do this exercise together, and work out a common, coherent, change strategy of Deals and Deadlines with them.

Chaos is not the same as full randomness. Your organisation's first pass through chaos is less risky if you're clear about which

'Attractors' your customers and associates share. The acceptance of organisational chaos will test the mettle of people who set out to meet their own challenges and deadlines. Chaos can't be controlled, but it can be strategically contained and limited beforehand. Anchor any key people early, to avoid 'talent bleeding'. According to a report by the Economist Intelligence Unit and Hewitt Associates, more than 1/3 of the 150 large international companies surveyed, reported the finding and retaining of talent, plus a lack of management capabilities, as the greatest obstacles to growth.[a]

Isolate those systems that you don't want to risk disrupting, in the wave effects of Perturbation. Estimate and scale any risks against what you absolutely cannot afford to lose. Expect to give 20 to 50 % of your time -the same holds for most Strategic Leaders – to major changes. Push more of your own current decision-making power downline, to liberate that time. Stop doing so many routine control checks. Create space for yourself. Successful business 'Mavericks' insist on one page reports with a cryptic newspaper style headline of the conclusions at the beginning. Find and share creative new ways to work smarter, not harder.

Check your own habits. What's the worst thing that could happen if you threw out most of your files? When do you really need to be in the office? Drop any excess baggage and travel light. The mechanical promise of high performance from instant new technology is seductive, but often unrealistic and inflexible.

High tech is no substitute for good people. Technology in organisations requires appropriate human values to operate well. New technology won't run effectively on old paradigms. It was massive team co-operation that put men on the moon and brought them back safely, not the computers.

Organisation is a weapon. Any competitive weapon should be sturdy, flexible, simple, and free of ornament. Product superiority is a rapidly copied myth today. A powerful unique organisation of fully committed and truly empowered people cannot be copied. Welcome diversity and difference before sameness and conformity. Values come before vision in times of chaos. Choose and invite your key people well from the start. Effective and vigorous change ability hangs on the successful nurturing and under-management of the entrepreneurial spirit and a deep respect

---

[a] We thank Arturo M. Garcia, Hassan Y. Awale & Petr Ulvr for this information.

for other people's success. Let the busy roots of the business constantly probe and breed trustworthy fruitful relationships, inside and out.

Part 5

HOW WILL THIS AFFECT YOUR JOB?

'Profound change makes terrible demands on leaders.' [a]

Section 3 explained how customers and entrepreneurs can transform a business organisation, from the inside out. Section 4 offered the PRO'T'US Lens, to observe, understand, and to sometimes intervene coherently, in the evolving nature of change in an organisation. This section first introduces the four roles of a change leader, then offers some exercises to help you to launch a change.

---

[a] Thomas A. Stewart, "Managing Change – How to Lead a Corporate Revolution", *Fortune* 28/11/94, p22

The Four Change Roles of a
Modern Business Leader

'There is a simpler way to lead organisations, one that requires less effort and produces less stress than the current practices.'
Margaret J. Wheatley

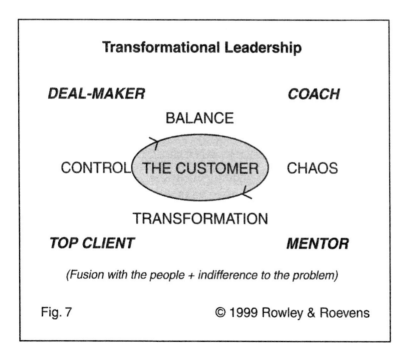

Transformational Leadership

DEAL-MAKER   *COACH*

BALANCE

CONTROL THE CUSTOMER   CHAOS

TRANSFORMATION

TOP CLIENT   *MENTOR*

(Fusion with the people + indifference to the problem)

Fig. 7   © 1999 Rowley & Roevens

Fusion with the people plus indifference to the problem means empowerment

'A vice president acts as a 'Godfather' to the group, but all of the actual work is directed by leaders below that rank and the group organizes itself as it sees fit....- management works out a contract with the team, after which it is turned loose.' [a]

Bob Eaton, former CEO, Chrysler

Executives must learn to stop being zoo keepers and become safari park rangers

Liberating people to reach their best natural performance levels means creating achievable target levels with them, that they fully intend to reach. At first this requires coaching by Leaders and Personnel experts. Once people are able to freely commit to deliver, then the safety net is removed. This major paradigm shift is crucial to a transformation. The individual, group, or organisation unit is then set free to self-organize, and is naturally expected to deliver to standard, and on time.

Strategic Change Leaders undergo four major role changes in precipitating this kind of transformation. These are:

- **Deal Maker**. Articulate the new vision and make strategic deals with individuals or teams.

- **Coach**. Listen, question and protect, to find ways to make all associates successful.

- **Mentor**. Inform, consult and share information. Present choices and options. Let people do things their own way. Admit you do not know. Budgets become investments. A

---

[a] *Fortune* 20/3/95, p95

trusted (but invited) strategic advisor, in a chain of deals and deadlines.

- **Top Client**. Accept only world class delivery. Build proud reputations.

Leaders may require some professional internal or outside help, to 'Train to Train' in:

- IT, Internet Economics & Diversity Management.
- Self-Organizing, Group & Network Dynamics.
- Entrepreneurship & Deal Making.
- Customer Focus.
- Wide Product Knowledge.

Don't allow managers to parachute in to sort out the mess

Use Pro'T'us to read any change situation strategically, as it is happening. Make as few interventions into the system as possible. Part of the exercise is to allow deliberate strategic Perturbation to spontaneously arise in parts of the old system, so you can expect many surprises; things falling apart (before they self-organize around customer attractors) and great variations in diversity, complexity and perplexity.

Fuse with the people but become indifferent to the problems

Once the deals are made, keep out of it. Don't ask to be informed of progress. The teams must own the pain of the problem to be motivated to find their own solutions. Offer really attractive performance incentives, make gifts of recognition and parade great examples. Light fires to Excite the energy levels to keep up the attack on the complexity of transformation. Support the people, but confidently expect them to deliver on their own promises.

2

Now Try These Exercises

– Alone, or individually among your change team.

EXERCISE 1. Task Centred Change – Think About Your Customers

Direct your mind to the practical issues & take time to complete the following:

A. What three to five specific things would you like to start doing in your firm?

1....

2....

3....

4....

5....

B. What three to five specific things would you like to stop doing in your firm?

1....

2....

3....

4...

5...

C. List some things that you would like to see happening spontaneously.

1...

2...

3...

4...

5...

Next, match some key people, around each activity:

A. Start doing involves:

1...

2...

3...

4...

5...

B. Stop doing involves:

1...

2...

3...

4...

5...

C. Happen Spontaneously might involve:

1...

2...

3...

4...

5...

The next step is to set up group meetings at various levels to discuss these specific items. Then define clear sets of tasks, offers, standards and deadlines. Finally, invite and agree who takes the responsibility to deliver. Now meet your people and talk it through

e.g.

Name(s)	Deal(s)	Delivery Date(s)
....	....	....
....	....	....
....	....	....
....	....	....
....	....	....

and so on...

(Note: Limits Can Often Betray Hidden Assumptions)

Surfacing and changing assumptions

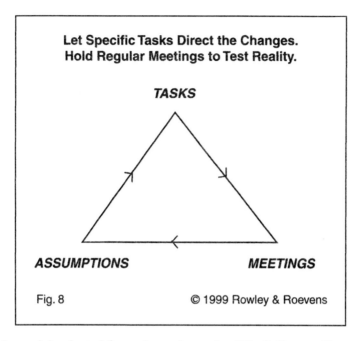

Let Specific Tasks Direct the Changes.
Hold Regular Meetings to Test Reality.

TASKS

ASSUMPTIONS   *MEETINGS*

Fig. 8   © 1999 Rowley & Roevens

This model, adapted from the early work of Prof. George Homens in the 1960s, shows the dynamic connection between three key aspects which influence human performance. Change any one and the other two will also change.

There Are Two Natural and Easily Accessible Ways To Change Assumptions:

* Re-framing someone's task, job title, or purpose can instantly change their behaviour.

* Physically bringing people together regularly, and informing them, changes their assumptions about each other and the purpose of their individual tasks linked to the real business of the enterprise.

EXERCISE 2. My own contribution to customer & competitor value?

Get together with your people and brainstorm to find the critical 8-10 things about your job that Customers love. These are the things you should do more of.

Then do the same exercise again to discover what your Competitors think you do poorly. These are the things you should do less of.

Then Brainstorm On the Firm's 8-10 Major Customer Values:

- *What is special about me/us?*
- *What does a total buying / using experience from us feel like for a customer?*
- *Why did they come to us?*
- *What's good and bad about us?*
- *Why do you think people give us their business?*
- *What makes us different from 'X', 'Y', 'Z' firms ... etc.?*

EXERCISE 3.Using The Strategic Change Lens

Think of some actions you have taken, or are about to take. Place these actions, with their possible effect on change. Do they:

- *Enhance?*
- *Perturb?*
- *Attract?*
- *Excite?*

Are these actions in the best coherent position in the spiral sequence?

EXERCISE 4. Some practical suggestions for building the new focus: The Mystery Customer Competitor Test

Draw up your own internal (8-10) customer-value list (see exercise 2). Test your own organisation and the competitors regularly.

- *Measure its effectiveness and report to your people.*
- *Build a customer-intimate database Together*
- *Make each customer famous in your firm.*
- *Build a customer fan club to tag their movements.*
- *Set up a central electronic customer/competitor database which everyone can access, and to which they can add new bits of information about key people or their staff, plus any signals of their changing business needs, or even of them changing their jobs! Have this information with you at the point of sale.*
- *Symbolically turn all associates into business representatives. Honda plants a tree when someone joins their organisation. Give everyone official company business cards with their own name, private address and the title Business Associate printed on it.*
- *Find creative ways for all people to symbolically put their own mark on the firm, and their particular work.*

CONCLUSION

First, a few parting words about customers. Initiating a change to allow better and more adaptively organized customer satisfaction to blossom, can give you a fast competitive edge, but it goes further. Change should nurture and foster a much more robust network strategy of long-term partnership building with everyone who touches, or is touched by, your business. The customer actually requires all of your people to work together, often far removed in time and space, from the point of sale. A first sale is simply a test of your organisation's ability to deliver. Repeat business rates and patterns should be studied closely, as valuable health indicators of a process which begins long before the point of sale, and can signal a stable loyal relationship of repeated business and happy customer references. This is the long term success measure of a business transformation. Customer success must come from the inside of every person in your firm. An adaptive or a generative business organisation grows inside its people, not the other way around. The real organisation question for management then becomes how to avoid anything in the structure that does not contribute, or actually blocks, the increase of customer value.

In the days of the Titanic, icebergs were often subject to naval escort attack, with explosives. Today's technology allows the navy to track and communicate their position and likely movement. By understanding the icebergs' behaviour, merchant ships can be safely left to simply avoid them. Once informed working people can clearly understand their own contribution to customer value in a business, they can also be safely left to navigate their own journey, and will likewise avoid any icebergs on the way.

Learning how to grow an evolving change is strategically quite simple, but operationally it's too complex to try to control centrally. Open information sharing and self-control is the key. Much of the complexity is best handled by fully committed individuals, working in multi-functional teams, who are close to the action. Like in the previously quoted example of Microsoft abruptly changing course for the internet, network information technology enabled the personal initiative of one lowly individual to quickly resonate, amplify, and reshape the emerging operational strategy of the whole enterprise, almost overnight.

> '...in the knowledge economy...only 15% of the working population physically touches their organisations' product whilst the other 85% add value through the creation, management and transfer of information.'[a]

Tending a dynamic web of innovative deals and deadlines, which maximise coincidence and stretch well informed, committed human beings, is a new executive challenge in many traditional industries. Organisations which seek to enable change rather than to constrain it, must learn to invite diversity, risk and opportunity. Only by accepting self-organizing chaos, can a business transformation reach deeply into the free market. Chaos is at the heart of global capitalism today, and we've all got to learn to live with it.

Best wishes,
Robin Rowley, Joseph Roevens,

---

[a] P. Sparrow & J. M. Hiltrop, *European HRM in Transition*, Prentice Hall, 1994, p93

Additional Notes and New Science Metaphors

Balance

Conventionally, the threshold of stability is the temporary outcome of a constant battle between the forces which tend to stabilize (energy flow) and those which tend to destabilize (energy transfers and blockages). In today's rapidly changing business environment, many firms are now firmly embedded in market conditions of non-equilibrium fluctuations, and full chaos. Rapport and sensitivity with this kind of environment is crucial to survival. As mentioned earlier in the text, when things change, you must also change, to stay the same.

Paradoxically therefore, stability comes from the ability to change imperceptibly and seamlessly with the environment, while instability stems from a reluctance or inability to change. In times of change, stability requires energy to flow freely, where instability blocks energy and increases entropy (see the definition of entropy, below).

Organisational stability now comes from fluctuations caused by responsive and committed customer contact, rapid feedback, high trust, open communications, innovation, and risk-taking. Instability arises through past successes, comfortable cash reserves and over-control, as well as by unexpected market fluctuations, predatory competitive action, rapid growth, and layoff's. Anything which damages people's ability to cooperate in an organisation's culture, destabilizes it operationally. Energy can collapse or become defensive. We think that long-term core instability happens in many organisations which downsize, re-engineer, or make similarly rational, but essentially old paradigm power and control based attempts, to try to change themselves.

In Chemistry, a process called 'catalytic feedback

amplification' happens when a sample of an element acts as a catalyst to create more of itself. Low trust, power, and over-control can grow organisationally, in much the same way. When viewed in these terms, there are many profitable firms in today's Fortune 500 whose increasing entropy does not represent a sound long-term investment. Permanent (hidden) instability, immobilizes a business organisation into heat death, not health.

Bifurcation

A system gets pushed over the threshold of stability by an excess or lack of a key element or substance. Things become unstable and start to fluctuate. The system reaches a self organizing B-point of maximum instability where it explores many possible states. Then it chooses. This is what happens in nature when a tree throws out a new branch. At the B-point, it is impossible to predict if the system will disintegrate into randomness, or leap to a higher level of order. The mixture of necessity and chance in a business organisation resembles the Dissipative Structures of Thermodynamics. These require more energy than the simpler systems which they replace. Thus, it is important not to collapse, or attempt to control the process, before self-organisation gets the chance to happen naturally around the Attractors. If an organisation is really going to transform, it is a much better strategy to Excite the turbulence of exploration.

Determinism breaks down at the B-point; outcomes become stochastic like tossing a coin, but in such non-equilibrium conditions order comes from fluctuations not probability. The past offers no guarantees for the future, because small changes can quickly produce big and often bizarre outcomes. Scenario Planners at Shell, were ready for the oil crisis, because they had contingency plans for wildly Bifurcating – possible but not likely – scenarios which had nothing to do with the normal gradual trends.

Non-equilibrium demands great sensitivity. It magnifies the

effects of tiny changes in the environment. Like the grain patterns in a piece of wood, the mix of necessity, capability, chance and choice, at the strategic B-points, describes the history of the system.

Change

According to Nobel Prize-winner Ilya Prigogine, only a small part of the universe is a closed mechanical system. Biological and social systems are open systems. They exchange energy, matter and information with the environment, continuously. Material reality is boiling with disorder and uncertainty. Change, not stability, is actually what's normal. That which is unnoticed has no name. Change is a concept built on the classical assumption of permanence. The word change may simply reflect a culture's measure of personal discomfort. Don't use it in your firm if it creates resistance.

Spontaneous changes in open systems, which evolve from chaos towards order and equilibrium, are quite unlike the deliberate changes caused, and controlled by the external manipulation of initial, intervening, or boundary conditions in closed systems. Continuous Change aims to transform a successful company into a successful company. You don't need to be sick to get better. You don't just need a crisis to move information and authority in an organisation.

Chaos

About 100 years ago Henri Poincaré emphasized a qualitative approach in Mechanics and researched the characteristics of chaotic systems. Chaos Theory, and its discipline & applications really started in the USA in the 1970's. Chaos is considered to be the essence of life. It lives where order merges into disorder and can be reached from either direction. Chaos is not Randomness. It is bounded (in maximum separation) by the influence of

Attractors,and was defined as a kind of order without periodicity by the scientist Hao Bai-Lin. Large systems (like the weather) tend towards disorder. According to Mitchell Feigenbaum, period rates of bifurcation double when a system moves towards chaos. It can go exponential fast. In Psychology, Chaos betokens a rapid change in beliefs (See Thomas Kuhn's paradigm shift). In business organisations, efficient Control should Attract creative Chaos, to self-organize.

Classical Science

Created by Galileo and Newton in the 17th and 18th Century, it was successful, and still persistently appeals to our limited sensory perception of reality today. The late Dr. David Bohm believed that science went beyond the mere accumulation of knowledge. It also shapes our perception and guides our actions.

Some basic assumptions of Classical Science are that:

- The system is closed, steady, and unchanging.
- Narrow artificial experimental conditions improve accuracy.
- Ceteris paribus, other things being equal, constants are standard and variables are isolated.
- A holistic complex process can be reduced and analysed in separate parts.
- The general rule is the most significant. Exceptions can be ignored.
- The Universe is precisely determined by its initial conditions.
- The spontaneous role of chance does not exist.
- Transformations are reversible and define the possibility of controlling a system.
- Given enough facts we can predict the future and reconstruct the past (Laplace).

Today, because of reconceptualisations about the way that

physical reality behaves and looks when you use more accurate measuring tools, these assumptions have mostly been replaced in science by Chaos Theory, Quantum Mechanics and Relativistic Physics. Natural systems are both random and irreversible. Also matter is not passive, but is now associated with processes of spontaneous self-organisation which produce order out of chaos. This takes us beyond the mathematics of mere space and time, and suggests that numbers may not be the only key to unlock the mysteries of the universe.

Contract

There are two types of business contract:

- Forcing – Do this and we'll pay, or, do that, e.g. Assembly workers, buyers and sellers.
- Incentive – Get good results, e.g. Owning shares is the ultimate incentive.

Control

Contra-rotulus (Latin – against the written scrolls).The formal authority to own and to command. After Bifurcating, a system may become stable and deterministic for a while. At this point in a business process, efficient control (only with commitment) can become a profitable production routine for a while. However, the effects of a rapid competitive response from anywhere in the world, increasingly tend to shorten these cycles.

There are five types of behaviour control in an organisation. These are :

- The formal power and authority system (mostly of rewards and punishment)
- The production pressure and flow chain
- The internal effects of the external market
- Self-organizing group and peer pressure

- Individual self-discipline, initiative, and motivation

Customer Focus – The Essential Rules:

- Under promise and over deliver
- Ask them what they want and give that service, those features, or those solutions.
- Give each customer one simple point of contact.
- Make relationship building gifts of information and tokens of recognition.
- Only say yes with integrity, and mean it.
- Relocate inspectors and close customer service departments.
- Invite all Associates to feel what the customer feels.
- Support internal customer advocates.
- Authorise everyone to get involved with complaints.
- Find out what the customer values and check your performance in each aspect.
- Evaluate and act to improve continuously.
- Get the right information into the right place and hands, on time.
- Change must release initiatives for new ways to help the customer.
- Reduce down time, accelerate cycles and offer special unique extras.
- Pay your Associates like business partners.
- Give everyone official company business cards.
- Benchmark the competition. Use the word customer more than they do.
- We all have customers, or we work for someone who does.
- Monitor all customer calls and orders each day on a public notice board.

The interaction of a business organisation with the changing outside world of customers, is a reflection of the global conditions of non-equilibrium which produce and support it. The system must be transformed to behave as a coherent whole, with each associate fully empowered, rewarded and informed to welcome this wider personal responsibility.

Energy

In Physics, energy is not actually produced, it is transferred from one place to another. In Psychology, it's wrong to think that you can directly motivate or energize somebody else, except by force. Imagination controls and directs human energy. An idea, or a particular display of values, can inspire new energy to manifest, as a vision transfers between people, but the widespread misconception of effective long-term psychological control (manipulation), just like the amoral term 'Human Resources', both rest on the similar values and assumptions of a mechanical, controlling and these days, quite obsolete science. The best kind of human energy is actually a gift, which conforms to moral laws. Celebrating the unique difference and variety between people, and taking full responsibility for your own actions, is not just the basis of human dignity, it is also the key to creative self-organizing behaviour. This is a key to understand the New Paradigm in business. Energy may dissipate on transfer, like heat tends to equalize its temperature. Force in this respect is dissipative, but pure randomness and chance are concentrative. Energy combined with chance can help to create balance in social systems.

Entrepreneur

A licensed value adding intermediary between the storehouses, characterised by initiative, freedom and purposeful energy.

Entropy

A concept first introduced by Clausius in 1865 to mathematically quantify disorder, it also extends to include mixing and randomness. Entropy increases only in the direction of the future. Due to the infinite information required, plus chance, a disorderly process cannot be reversed back, in the same way that it arrived, to reconstitute order. We cannot produce situations that would return us to our past. This is also called the entropy barrier.

Entropy production expresses the irreversible changes which happen in relation to the spontaneous evolution of a system. Entropy flow depends on whether the system is closed (i.e. zero flow), or open. When increasing entropy reaches a maximum point of equilibrium, the system arrives at a state known as heat death. Once diversity no longer exists to distinguish the past from the present, theoretically, time vanishes.

According to The Second Law Of Thermodynamics, this is the ultimate fate of our universe. Because everything in the universe tends towards disorder, entropy always increases. Some scientists now accept that this may only apply in isolated closed systems which are devoid of life. Life continuously evolves towards higher levels of order and organisation, precisely through disorderly spontaneous processes, natural selection and self-organisation. As some systems run down or disintegrate, others grow more coherent. Entropy thus acts like an Attractor only in a few closed systems. '...thermodynamic entropy fails miserably as a measure of the changing degree of form and formlessness in the creation...of complex information systems like the brain...The important laws, the creative laws, lie elsewhere.' (James Gleick. Op.cit.:318)

Evolution

This is Nature's process of exploring the alternatives, which lead to the spontaneous selection of rare events. Evolution produces a succession of irreversible social and biological bifurcations (mutations) by constantly approaching and testing a random future. It recognises space, shuns limits and constraints, and advances at the slightest opportunity. Traffic is a good example.

Goal strategy focuses inwards on individual ability, where a limit strategy looks more at the state of the environment. Even if they exist, the purpose, goals, time scale, or destination of Evolution are unknowable. Its path can only be seen upon arrival.

Evolution is an impeccable servant to the next generation of the living. It does not allow a final state to be less attractive than an initial state. Only what already works, may improve. Such perfect integrity stems from an absolute indifference towards changes in the present. Evolution grants the time to experience randomness, but denies any organism (except cancer) immortality.

Feedback

Simple feedback systems are one dimensional, like a thermostat. Complex Feedback loops amplify fluctuations. The faster communication takes place within a system, the greater will be the percentage of unsuccessful fluctuations, and thus, the more stable the system. Communication leads to improved systems integration and stability. In unstable conditions which demand sensitivity to the environment, up-line and lateral feedback enables self organisation, in three dimensions.

Fractal

A picture of a chaotic Attractor. The shape of one detail resembles the whole. It's a pattern which repeats in a similar way, but is never quite the same.

Intuition

This means listening to your mind instead of talking to it, and taking special notice of accidents or, coincidences. As a direct vision of the mind, by the mind, our intuition is also essential to the perception of such things as duration, spirit, and change (after Bergson). Intuition cannot produce the system, only the result.

Learning

There are two types of learning :

- Adaptive – For coping with the present. This is usually rational and analytical.
- Generative – To create and expand future capabilities. This is inspirational, visionary, playful and intuitive.

Change requires both a learning organisation, and a forgetting organisation too.

Open Systems

Describes organisations which transform environmental energy, information and material constantly, by direct contact, self-organisation, feedback and spontaneous exploration.

Order

The chain towards disorder runs from:

- Stasis (crystal)
- Consistency
- Periodicity
- Chaos
- Full Randomness (disorderly liquid and gas).

Paradigm

Knowing how to look. Thomas Kuhn realized in 1947 how patterns, and metaphors, totally influence our perception of reality. Paradigms do not gradually change, they can shift dramatically according to the introduction of new information and experience.

Newton's three hundred year old Mechanical Paradigm of the universe to which Descartes, Locke and Bacon also subscribed, shifted in Physics in the 1920's. Western Management sciences, dominated by predictability, order, control, and arrow time, are still mostly unconsciously using it. A New Paradigm of business organisation is emerging.

Quantum Mechanics

There is no scientific objective reality. Position and momentum are not independent variables as in Classical Mechanics

Resistance

Considered a natural part of the change process which requires sensitivity by management. The main fear today is usually about you losing your job, not the ability to cope with changes. When reconciling the terminally ill to the fact that they are dying, they often go through the following steps: – Disbelief, – Anger, – Negotiation, -Depression, – Acceptance

Aggression is not the only choice of behaviour when you are angry. The typical causes of aggression are:

- Loss of possession
- Intruders
- Frustration
- Control of space
- Access to Breeding
- Dominance
- Betrayal.

Self-Organisation

Order and organisation can arise spontaneously through this process. Such uniformity and polarisation defies classical Physics and Probability Theory.

Silence

Is a good listener, a fine answer, and a great teacher. It is also a powerful negative intervention. Silence at the top creates noise at the bottom.

Time

Aristotle considered time to be the measure of change. Einstein showed that it was relatively elastic. Some Physicists think that time is a function of entropy, and only appears when sufficient diversity exists to make the past and the future irreversible.

It is known in space exploration that time is measurably affected by gravity and also by high speed travel (you experience less time as you go faster). Classical mechanics considered that, given enough information, time was reversible. Most scientists reject this notion today.

There are four basic world cultural models of time. These are:

- Arrow time of past, present and future. This measures progress and results.
- Sidereal or the circular time of the planets. Hopefully, the sun will rise tomorrow.
- Zero – The future comes to us. We track our path in an already complete universe.
- Unique – Each measure of irreversible existence is not exactly like any other.

Is time therefore a linear particle event, a periodic wave phenomenon, a subjective illusion, or a fractal, or all of these, and more? Prigogine suggests that biological systems, may have been selected, or rejected, as a result of their own unique past, to generate specific kinds of organisation processes, and that time's irreversibility is the mechanism that brings order out of chaos.

Transformation

Transformation begins when you realize that you have lost your way. It produces irreversible changes in how a problem, or a situation, is perceived. Once desire conquers need as a motivator, you're dealing with entrepreneurs. Continuously transform Purpose, Products, Processes and Performance.

Turbulence

To perceive the order in a turbulent river depends upon how closely you look at it. From a distance it appears to be irregular or chaotic, but close up it reveals the highly organized coherent behaviour, of millions and millions of molecules. The transition from a steady flow to turbulence, is actually a process of self-organisation.

Profiles of the Authors

Robin Michael Rowley lectures, researches and coaches in Organisation Transformation. Mr. Rowley has thirty five years experience in Industrial Relations, Organisation Development and Change. After working in the Industrial Relations Division of Kodak Ltd., in 1974 Mr. Rowley became a Senior Lecturer at London University. He was an early pioneer of Self-Directed Teamwork and Organisation Change, running programmes for such organisations as: Ford, Marconi, ICI, English Electric and the British Armed Forces. Now resident in Belgium, Robin Rowley is a Faculty Professor of Organisation Behaviour in Brussels and Antwerp, and is a visiting lecturer at The Universities of: Humberside, Breda, Gent, Antwerp, and Prague. He holds post-graduate diplomas in Business Management, plus a Master's degree in Industrial Relations from the University of Salford in England.

Joseph Janaprya Roevens started business life as a European Union lobbyist, promoting organisations which are dedicated to ecological values and healthy market performance, such as Ecover nv, a leading ecological detergent manufacturer. Mr Roevens lectures, researches and trains Cross-cultural Management, HRM, Strategy and Ethics at Breda University of Applied Science – NHTV, Fachhochschule Bremerhaven and private clients. Joseph holds post-graduate degrees in Economics, Education and International Management from Cornell, Johns Hopkins, IEP-HEC (Paris) and Tilburg University. He is a member of the Golden Key National Honor Society (USA) and received Kenneth Blanchard's Leadership Eagle Award. Follow Joseph's work on http://organizewithchaos.blogspot.com.

Index